ALL OUR YESTERDAYS

All Our Yesterdays

Childhood memories from across the ages

compiled and edited by

Gervase Phinn

Dalesman

First published in 2008 by Dalesman
an imprint of
Country Publications Ltd
The Water Mill
Broughton Hall
Skipton
North Yorkshire
BD23 3AG

Reprinted 2008, 2009

ISBN 978-1-85568-253-5

Printed by 1010 Printing

Frontispiece: Gervase Phinn aged six

Contents

Preface

Putting together this book has been a labour of love. I have so much enjoyed reading and selecting the fascinating stories, anecdotes, thoughts, poems, reminiscences and photographs which make up this wonderful and unique collection about children and childhood.

I am greatly indebted to all the contributors to this book but would like to mention four very special people without whose help, encouragement, hard work and advice *All Our Yesterdays* would never have seen the light of day. Firstly my thanks go to Robert Flanagan, managing director of Country Publications, who has always kept faith with my various projects. I should like to thank him, too, for the very generous donation from proceeds of this book to Hurdles, a charity which enables disabled children to lead more enjoyable and fulfilled lives. Ever-cheerful and efficient Linda McFadzean has done a huge amount of work behind the scenes, typing up the extracts and organising and securing permissions, and she too deserves my gratitude. Phil Sootheran has used his design and digital skills to create such striking photographs. Finally I should like to thank my editor, Mark Whitley who has, with great patience and unstinting energy, guided and co-ordinated the task of creating this book.

Gervase Phinn

Introduction

On literary lunches I sometimes meet writers who have come from the most dreadful homes and experienced the most harrowing childhoods, with cold, cruel parents who neglected or abused them and who told them frequently how very disappointed they were in them.

One only has to read the blurb on the back covers of the many biographies and autobiographies which line the bookshop shelves to appreciate what difficult, miserable and sometimes unbearable lives some people have led as children. In the large bookshops now there is a section devoted entirely to 'Tragic Life Stories' or 'Misery Memoirs'.

I thank God that my childhood was so very different. It was joyous. Growing up, I imagined that all children had loving, amusing, supportive parents like mine, who wanted the very best for their children, who read to them every night, talked with them, sang to them, laughed with them. My life was full of happiness and conversation, music and books.

There is a view that those of us who had a pretty ordinary, uneventful and happy childhood really have nothing much to write about.

"When I look back on my childhood," writes Frank McCourt in *Angela's Ashes: a Memoir of Childhood*, "I wonder how I managed to survive it at all. It was, of course, a miserable childhood: the happy childhood is hardly worthwhile."

Well, in this rich and varied anthology of anecdotes, firsthand accounts, stories, poems and reminiscences, the reader will soon appreciate that 'the ordinary childhoods' described in these pages can not only be very happy and full of humour

and insight, but have been most certainly worthwhile and
worthy to be shared with others.

Gervase Phinn

1. HOME

When I was young I thought that all children had fathers and mothers like mine: loving, funny, generous, ever-supportive.

I thought all children had mothers who took out their false teeth and pretended to be witches, and fathers who told wild and wonderful stories, and pretended to be monsters and chased them around the living room growling and grunting.

I imagined that all homes had books and stories, music and laughter, courtesy and good manners, honesty and love.

It is only now I am older, and have met countless numbers of children in the schools I have visited, that I appreciate just how special my home was and how hard my parents tried to bring up the four of us, in that modest red-brick semi in Rotherham, to be honest and decent young people.

Now, in later life, I know for sure that the relationship between a child and his or her parents is the most critical influence on that child's life.

I remember once, when I was six and we were on holiday in Blackpool, I wet the bed. Mum had told me not to drink too much that evening but I had carried on downing a good few glasses of cherryade.

"You'll be sorry," she said, and left it at that.

I was indeed sorry because I awoke in the middle of the night distraught to find my pyjamas sopping and a warm wet patch in the middle of the bed.

There were no recriminations.

"Don't get all upset," said Mum, giving me a cuddle. "We all wet the bed at some time in our lives. It's not the end of the world. Accidents happen."

The child was a keen bed-wetter. Noel Coward

She washed me, changed me, put me in a clean pair of pyjamas and popped me in her bed next to Dad. I slept between my parents that night, and felt safe and secure and loved.

My father was typical of many Yorkshire folk: industrious, plain-speaking, generous and good-humoured, with strong views and a wry sense of humour.

After coming out of the army (he was a despatch rider with the Royal Artillery) he became a steelworker at the great foundry of Steel, Peach and Tozer.

As a boy, on my way to watch Sheffield United, I remember well the bumpy bus ride from Rotherham to Sheffield via Attercliffe, past the place where he worked for thirty or more years. Down the depressing Don Valley rattled the blue and white double-decker bus, past dirty corrugated iron sheds, yards of scrap, rusty cranes and huge overhead transporters. It was an area that contained little but dust, dirt and an incredible ugliness.

Years later, when I visited the magnificent Magna, the industrial museum now sited in the Don Valley, it was only then that I fully realised what an unpleasant and dangerous job my father had, and what a very special man he must have been to have gone into that hell day after day, night after night, and never complain.

Most of us want a job which offers some variety and challenge — to go into work in the morning and look forward to something different. But the steelworker had to go into work day after day with the same predictable, monotonous and intensely dirty job to do.

And the fact that my father did that job without moaning or getting moody or angry with us children seems to me to be remarkable.

Gervase Phinn

Children sweeten labours; but they make misfortunes

The first thing I remember is sitting in a pram at the top of a hill with a dead dog lying at my feet.

Graham Greene

We were a happy family — we always had shoes.

Ernie Wise

Insignificant is not a word many people would choose to describe me but it applied to me in the early days of my childhood, which I adored in all its aspects. If anybody should be grateful for their upbringing, for their mam and dad, I'm that person. I was the kid who came from a little part of paradise.

Brian Clough

The smell of the baking bread was the most attractive of our household aromas. Dad's wind the least.

Tom Courtenay

The Mitchells, rising dizzily from c2 to c1 and moving an unprecedented distance from Halifax to Baildon, were neither summat nor nowt; upwardly mobile because where my grandparents had rented a terrace, my parents started out in a 1930s semi (costing £350, with my dad worrying into the 1950s about the repayments), but downwardly living. I went to Woodbottom Council School, and in clogs too, though tiptoeing down a tarmac street rather than clattering down cobbles so as not to draw attention to a shame I soon managed to get rid of.

Austin Mitchell

Mexborough was a friendly place, a mining town with lots of pits in the area. One of my earliest memories as a boy was hearing the sound of the miners who wore clogs and walked to work. They'd meet up at street corners. There'd then be

more bitter. Sir Francis Bacon

Gie a bairn his will, 'an a whelp his fill,

more and more of footsteps. Clink, clink, clink — they made a distinctive noise on the road. They had a 'snap can' and a 'dudley' full of water with a cork, which gurgled as they walked.

Peter Roy

Apart from the number on the door it was indistinguishable from any other red-brick, terraced house in the neighbour-hood: a Coal Board house with two small rooms downstairs and three smaller ones above. As houses go, it wasn't much to write to the National Trust about. But it was home, which was infinitely more important. A place of warmth and caring, a little part of a true community, which seems hopelessly out-moded and old-fashioned now but which was in many ways better than the society which is overtaking and replacing it.

I may have moved away from Fitzwilliam but I have never grown apart from its people or the memories. I couldn't even if I wanted to.

Geoffrey Boycott

I was well aware of the social stigma of our poverty. Even the poorest of children sat down to a home-cooked Sunday dinner. A roast at home meant respectability, a ritual that distin-guished one poor class from another. Those who could not sit down to Sunday dinner at home were of the mendicant class, and we were that. Mother would send me to the nearest coffee-shop to buy a sixpenny dinner (meat and two vegetables). The shame of it — especially on Sunday! I would harry her for not preparing something at home, and she would vainly try to explain that cooking at home would cost twice as much.

Charlie Chaplin

I can remember on one occasion Mam baking a loaf of bread and telling me that it was the only thing we had to eat in the

an' neither will do weel. Scottish proverb

house. Then a neighbour came round and told us that they did not have a single scrap of food in the house, so Mam gave her half of our loaf.

Patricia Cluderay

My mother's thrift was a powerful factor in keeping us afloat, and other people's deprivation could sometimes surprise even her. She told of once going to visit my father's half-sister in Darton, a mining village near Barnsley. They had just finished their Sunday dinner when there was a knock on the door. A small boy stood there with a message: "Me mam says can we borrow your joint."

The joint was tolerantly handed over and brought back a little later minus the slices with which the neighbours had made their meal.

Stan Barstow

Fish and chips made us what we are; overweight slobs. It was school dinners and works canteen, the 'chip oil' our reunion, and fish and chips at home our parliament. In generous moments we even bought them for girls — cakes you understand, not fish — but if you didn't click at the New Vic or Saltaire (as I didn't), a packet of fish and chips on the way home was the consolation prize, and hotter than the girls.

Austin Mitchell MP

We ate a lot of rice pudding. Mother would put a pint of milk into a pudding and bake it in the oven with a grating of nutmeg and a flavouring of vanilla. Does that make your mouth water? It does mine.

Eric Morecambe

When at home she [Emily Brontë] took the principal part of the cooking upon herself, and did all the household ironing;

A baby is nothing more than a loud noise at one end

and after Tabby grew old and infirm it was Emily who made all the bread for the family; and anyone passing by the kitchen door might have seen her studying German out of an open book, propped up before her, as she kneaded the dough; but no study, however interesting, interfered with the goodness of the bread, which was always light and excellent.

Mrs Gaskell

Growing up in Dublin in the 1950s, I was in love with Marlon Brando. I sent fan letters. I wanted him to come to Ireland, to fall in love with our country and with me. We would, of course, marry and live happily ever after.

But I prayed he wouldn't arrive on a Friday, as that was the day our house smelled of fish. You see, in those days, you couldn't possibly eat meat on a Friday or you would burn in hell. We crouched in fear of being somewhere away from home and eating meat on Friday inadvertently. And however badly we cooked meat, I can't tell you what a disaster we made of fish.

Living as we do on a beautiful island whose seas, rivers, and lakes leap with gorgeous fish, did we cook nice fish for ourselves? No, we did not. Fish were meant to be a penance, and they were cooked penitentially.

Maeve Binchy

Children did not know the worth of money then, for there were no shops nearer than eight miles away. We would get a few boiled sweets when one of the boats sailed across to Grimsby taking their crabs to market there. The sailors took a bag and list from each housewife of groceries that were needed.

George A Jarratt

I remember going to a sweet shop the day sweets came off ration and buying about six different varieties of sweets just because I had never been able to do it before.

Irene Abrahams

and no sense of responsibility at the other. Ronald Knox

A favourite, ie inexpensive, chew which has now virtually disappeared was the tiger nut. This fibrous morsel could be described as resembling an owl pellet dropped by a constipated bird which had been feeding solely on the insides of horsehair mattresses and the tufts on top of coconuts, with perhaps a beakful of haircord carpet for pud. You chewed and chewed your tiger nut but it yielded little flavour and did not diminish as the hours went by. I cannot say I miss it.

Frank Muir

At Woodhead & Sons, sugar was in huge open sacks, with a scoop to feed the sweet contents into stiff blue paper bags. Butter was uncovered in a huge mound with wooden spatulas to pat the creamy slabs into the required weight. Hams hung from ceiling hooks above a huge cheese which was sliced into portions with a wire. There was one case with polonies, penny ducks, sausages, black puddings, bacon joints ready for the slicer, meat pies of all sizes and huge jars of pickles.

There were well-filled flypapers curling from the roof with insects adhering to the sticky surfaces. There was always a distinct odour of paraffin, coal bricks, firelighters, and firewood with loops of wire holding the bundles of sticks together.

There was sawdust on the floor, and clouds of dust rose at the end of the day when the premises were swept by Mr Woodhead.

John Morgan

Penny ducks were made from all sorts of innards, little bits of this and that, with an onion and a little rusk and seasoning. The mixture was put into a large square baking tin, sectioned off, and baked. Then, with some gravy which we used to make too, people used to come with a white porcelain basin for the gravy, saying "A penny duck or two, please," which you'd hand them on a square of grease-proof paper.

Peter Roy

Like so many infants of tender years, he presented to the eye the aspect

of a mass murderer suffering from an ingrowing toenail. P G Wodehouse

My father tells of how, when unexpected visitors arrived at home and he was small, Elizabeth, their old servant, would take the shotgun and march off into the rookery behind the house, there to shoot a couple of rooks. She would be halfway through the preparation of a rook pie when my grandmother went to see what could be provided, at short notice, for tea.

E M J Reid

We used to eat fresh turnips while feeding the cows and even tried cow cake with treacle — yuk!

John Iveson

The railway came but the people in Whitby didn't go. What would they go for? There was nowhere to go.

Mary Jane Dryden

One Friday as we were coming out of school, a man was distributing leaflets advertising 'Animated Pictures'. I asked for two pence and went to see them next day.

There was a quick, jerky comic picture of a man chasing a mouse all over a woman's bedroom, while she jumped about hysterically. The man caught it, and the woman got into bed, when the mouse escaped again and, streaking up the foot of the bed and over the bedclothes, ran right into the woman's mouth, which she had opened wide to scream.

Someone's idea of a joke! The pity of it was, I went home and told them. Mother, who slept with her mouth open, at once decided to move — because of the mice. Father protested, and said he would soon put the mice down. They were only fieldmice which had got in when the house was standing empty and would soon leave. But Mother refused to stay in a house troubled with mice after I had told her about the film, and so we were soon on the move to another part of town

May Crewe

The thing that impresses me most about America is the way

Every day, without fail, my mother would undo our plaits and comb through our hair with a small-tooth comb. If we so much as scratched our heads, she would stop whatever she was doing and look to see if we had picked up anything.

Grace Foakes

At twelve or so the children started in the mill as half-timers, graduating to full time within a year or two. Lil and her eldest sister also had to help in the home and with the younger children, for Lil's mother had a faulty heart.

One day it fell to Lil's lot to make her first Yorkshire pudding for their family of eight. After more than an hour in the oven, the pudding was discovered boiling merrily. On being asked how much flour she had put in the mixture, Lil replied: "Just a bit in t' bottom o' t' basin."

Then there was the laundry class. "Bring something to iron next week," said the instructor, and every one duly turned up with the usual small article — except Lil. She appeared carrying a clothes basket full to the brim with a week's ironing for eight.

I Greaves

I was born in the shadow of the everlasting hills. My earliest excursions and adventures were on the heathery hillsides amid old alum-and-jet workings and in the sloping woodlands in which foxes and badgers (not to mention adders) abounded.

The first horse I ever bought was from a dales farmer. The first packs of foxhounds and harriers with which I hunted were the Bilsdale, the Farndale and the Glaisdale, and number one of a fairly hefty list of books I have written was about dalesmen and their love of sport.

As I have said, I was born a hill-man, and if the tang of heathery heights is in your blood, if the smell of burning peat was in your infant nostrils, if as a child you learned where ravens built, where vipers slept, in which ravines were caves

parents obey their children. Edward, Duke of Windsor

We were put to Dickens as children but it never quite took. The

tenanted by cats you thought were wild, but were only degen-
erate domesticated feline poachers obsessed by blood lust, if
you had early come under the humbling spell of the immensi-
ty of mountains and the vastness of sweeping moorland... I
say when all these are the heritage of man or woman, he or
she, like a homing pigeon, never forgets, and never loses the
urge to return to that spiritual-home 'heaf' where is a combi-
nation of grandeur, peace, poetry, music and abiding content.

J Fairfax-Blakeborough

It was my job to hold the cows' tails during milking and I
often went home covered in 'offerings' from skitty cows feeding on green pasture.

John Iveson

Although I grew up in a town, my Dad was a true country-
man. As soon as I was old enough, he taught me the names of
flowers and trees, animals, birds and insects. Once we got a
car, we went out into the country every Sunday and I always
found something for the school nature table, such as catkins,
a disused birds' nest, a pheasant's tail-feather, autumn leaves
and acorns.

The interest stayed and, fifty years on, I still can't resist
picking up pine cones and conkers every autumn.

Hazel Mary Martell

Nobody doubted that our arrival had improved the tone of the
neighbourhood. The previous tenants of number 174 had, we
were told, gone to the Horse and Jockey pub every night, leaving their children to amuse themselves with hammers and
nails. When we moved in, the skirting boards and the door
jambs were riddled with holes as if they had been ravaged by
giant woodworm.

Roy Hattersley

unremitting humanity soon had me cheesed off. Alan Bennett

My friend John Finch, creator of the TV series *A Family at War* and *Sam*, once had it put to him by a colleague: "I don't think you've ever known real poverty, John".

"Oh, yes, I have", Finch replied; "but I've never known squalor".

For my part, I didn't like squalor then and I like it even less when it is accompanied by wealth or an arty-farty preoccupation with higher things than the simple matter of keeping clean.

Stan Barstow

We had simple needs and pleasures. To see a car round our village was something of an event. The thrill to be had here was in seeing a car whose make and marque was unfamiliar to us. Such as the car of a travelling salesman from a faraway place as Leeds or Rotherham.

Fred Trueman

Mam kept an eye on our size. She was keen on measuring us, marking the wall with a pencil. Getting measured was one of the highlights of the month because she associated no malnutrition in our house.

Brian Clough

I always think how happy we were. We didn't have a lot of stress like you do nowadays. The secret was that nobody was better than anybody else and nobody tried to be.

We were all in the same boat. I think that's why people helped one another so much. If anybody died or was ill, everybody helped out because they were all alike.

It was a kind of insurance — if you helped then, they helped you. I don't think they looked on it like that, but that's what it was.

Mary Jane Dryden

Children and zip fasteners do not respond

to force ... except occasionally. Katherine Whitehorn

Perhaps the greatest social service that can be rendered by anybody to the

The day is overcast with slanting needles of sleet. Pools of yesterday's rain mark the place where I believe their terraced house was situated. I stare at my unfocused reflection in the murky, shimmering pools and look for other faces. The spontaneous, uncomplicated memories of childhood come back. There is a short, gloomy passageway from the front door. A barely furnished and unused front room is northward-facing, making it cold and sunless like a mausoleum. A back room, brightened a little by light from a single gas-mantle, is the main living area, with its slab-like stone sink that stands like an altar in front of a net-curtained sash window. A glowing fire provides heat for an oven, and from behind its heavy door come savoury cooking smells. These mingle with a heady, rich aroma of Twist tobacco from Grandfather Tom's pipe. A thick tablecloth with tassels, like a blanket, covers a table. There are a handful of ornaments: some have faded patterns and are veined with age. I'm surrounded by an aura of contentment in this room which I readily accept, take childlike comfort in and do not attempt to understand.

George Sweeting

In many ways I was lucky to experience a sense of belonging and togetherness, which seems to have been lost in so much of life nowadays. We had never heard of community spirit — that's the sort of catch-phrase which seems most used when genuine community spirit is missing. Our sense of community was spontaneous. It was simply a way of life.

Geoffrey Boycott

---

country and to mankind is to bring up a family. George Bernard Shaw

2. PARENTS

My earliest memory of my mother was sitting at the kitchen table making gingerbread men. The gingerbread men in Graftons Bakery in Rotherham all looked exactly alike and formed from a template. Mine were individuals. Some had large ears, others long noses, some small, others fat and squat, and some had long, thin legs and spidery arms.

I remember stirring the light brown mixture in the large white pot bowl and then forming the figures, pressing in the currants for the eyes and nipples and tummy buttons. With a large wooden spoon I would scrape out the bowl as I waited for the Gingerbread Men to cook. Then they appeared from the oven arranged on a tray and I would line them up like soldiers. I was always loath to eat them. Mum would then chant:

Run, run as fast as you can
You can't catch me,
I'm the Gingerbread Man!

She would always put aside two or three of the biscuits, wrap them in greaseproof paper and put them in her bag. I knew where they were going.

Mum trained as a state-registered nurse and state-certified midwife, and by the time I arrived on the scene she had been promoted from school nurse to become a health visitor touring homes in Canklow. Her 'patch', the place where her mother was born, was still a dark and disadvantaged area of the town, densely packed with row after row of mean back to back redbrick terraces. The gingerbread men she put in her

Where does the family start? It starts with a young man falling in love

bag were for certain children she came across on her visits to Canklow.

Very often I would search through my toy cupboard for a Dinky car or a lead soldier, for a ball or a game, only to be told by Mum: "It's gone to Canklow'. It was the same with clothes. My brother Michael would ask where a particular tie had gone. or Alex, my other brother, would comment on the disappearance of his favourite shirt, to receive the predictable reply: "It's gone to Canklow." Soon we became so used to hearing the familiar phrase that Mum would start: "It's..." and we would all chorus: "gone to Canklow".

My sense of humour, such as it is, indeed my sense of fun, was nurtured by my father, who always maintained that life was too short to be taken seriously. He loved to tell jokes and he could tell them well. He had the comic's sense of timing and could create the most wonderfully amusing facial expressions. He was good with accents too, and was a superb mimic. He would recite monologues that I know by heart to this day — 'Albert and the Lion', 'The Green Eye of the Little Yellow God,' 'The Boy Stood on the Burning Deck' — and could tell the most enthralling stories. As a child I swam in an ocean of language.

Gervase Phinn

———————

I remember my parents' simple ways, gentle humility and an absence of a strong acquisitive instinct in their lives.

George Sweeting

I told my father that I had just read a book by Bernard Shaw. He stopped still in the path where we were walking and said: "I have heard of other people having children like that, but I have always prayed God I might be spared."

Stephen Spender

with a girl — no superior alternative has yet been found. Winston Churchill

My father was not himself up to being criminal in a big way, but he was lost if he couldn't cheat in a small way: so much of his pleasure derived from it. I grew up thinking it absolutely normal that most Englishmen were like this. I still suspect that's the case.

Blake Morrison

A Dalesman to His Son

Well, lad,
I'll tell thee summat:
Life for me an't been no easy road to walk.
It's been a long hard journey —
Mostly uphill all the way.
At times it's been a hot and dusty trail,
Wi' potholes and sharp stones beneath mi feet
And a sweltering sun burning the back o' mi neck.
Sometimes it's been knee-deep wi' mud
And thick wi' snow and blocked wi' fallen trees,
With an icy wind blowing full in mi face.
There were times when it's been dark and dangerous
And I've been lonely and afraid and felt like turning back.
But all the time, lad,
I've kept plodding on,
And climbing stiles,
And scaling walls,
And seeing signposts,
And reaching milestones,
And making headway.
So, lad, don't you turn round,
Don't go back on the road
For I'm still walking,
I'm still walking,
And life for me an't been no easy road to walk.

Gervase Phinn

My parents were very pleased that I was in the army. The fact

that I hated it somehow pleased them even more. Barry Humphries

Every luxury was lavished on you —

They were hard but happy days. Families depended on each other. Neighbours helped to peg out the washing. If the lady of the house was 'confined', she could rely on the folk next door to make her home ship-shape for the arrival of the doctor and midwife for the everyday occurrence — another home delivery of another new baby.

People were kind and considerate. They shared each other's joys, blessings and tragedies. They celebrated births and they mourned at the wakes — those mysterious nocturnal gatherings where prayers were chanted and vigils kept before the remains of a loved one were taken to the local church for a service prior to burial.

John Morgan

I was the product of a working-class generation that possessed little in the way of expectation. I had been brought up in a family and a community where we were taught not to have great hopes, because invariably that would result in disappointment. In the main most men worked in the pits, in agriculture as farmhands, or in manual labour. No one I knew ever aspired to do anything different. Young people simply accepted that they too would embark upon such work for the rest of their lives. Which explains why, rather than being a cricketer for Yorkshire, my ambition was to become a bricklayer.

Fred Trueman

When I was a boy I lived on a farm seven miles east of York. If, when the eggs were gathered, there happened to be any very small ones among them, they were left on a windowsill behind the house, as it was considered unlucky to take them inside. My father used to throw them over the roof, but before he did so he sent one of us to the end of the house to warn him should anyone be at the front.

W M Hudson

atheism, breastfeeding, circumcision. Joe Orton

Eggs are not all they are cracked up to be, and they certainly were not over sixty years ago when the first cargo of the dried variety arrived in starving wartime Britain.

My mother became a dab hand at whisking dried eggs into a consistency ready for frying, although she had problems when she embarked on more ambitious concoctions. Her dried egg custards had a strange effect on the pastry. The base always floated to the top of the mixture, and we had to eat a type of baked upside-down pudding.

They were one of her few culinary failures, and another was a dried egg crème brûlée, although I must admit you didn't get many of those on our estate.

John Morgan

I remember with shame Dad's brief spell as a dustman (or as he put it, a refuse collector). They called at our school one play-time. In an agony of embarrassment, I saw Dad clattering the dustbins across the playground, cursing grandly and singing in his resonant voice. I pretended I hadn't seen him and Dad never forgave me.

Nicholas Charles

My father does not like waiting in queues. He is used to patients waiting in queues to see him, but he is not used to waiting in queues himself. A queue, to him, means a man being denied the right to be where he wants to be at a time of his own choosing, which is at the front, now.

Blake Morrison

In the 1950s, my Dad did the football pools and one week he won the first dividend. When the cheque arrived, it was for £128 — quite a lot of money in those days. With it, Dad treated ten of us to Sunday lunch and bought a new television. He also achieved one of his own ambitions by ordering a pair of

Parents can only give good advice or put them on the right paths, but the

hand-made shoes. He never won as much again, but for that one weekend we were millionaires.

Hazel Martell

Dad was tall. He was a lean 6 feet 1½ inches and he was gifted with accomplishments that were dazzlingly impressive to a small son: he could cut hair, repair socks, name the stars, do a little tap-dancing, and he never lost his temper or shouted or complained. He was also rather good-looking, as was my mother. I am allowed to say this because physical traits notoriously jump a generation.

Frank Muir

The pièce-de-résistance was my father's bicycle, on which he had cycled some hundreds of miles with my mother. It had a fixed wheel, a naked chain, a lamp and tool bag by way of accessories. Every spring my father re-enamelled it, cleaned the handlebars, and contemplated selling it. Always it returned to its place against the wall. Its memories were too precious.

E M J Reid

He was kind of a Victorian father. He had his own chair near the coal fire — miners got their coal at a very nominal cost — and nobody had to touch him as they went past. If we accidentally kicked his foot or something, he'd go for us, not physically (and he imitated growling imprecations).

If he didn't like some food my mother gave him, he would say, "I'll throw this back o' t' fire."

My mother would say, "All right, go on."

He never did. She called his bluff.

He was a conscientious father who wanted his children not to have the suffering, the drawbacks and the restricted life he'd had, and he saw that we didn't.

Henry Moore

final forming of a person's character lies in their own hands. Anne Frank

In his dressing-gown, with his whip in his hand, he [father] attended our breakfast ... that disgusting milk! He began with me; my beseeching look was answered by a sharp cut, followed by as many more as were necessary to empty the basin; Jane obeyed at once, and William after one good hint. They suffered less than I did; William cared less, he did not enjoy his breakfast, but he could take it; Jane always got rid of it [by vomiting].

Elizabeth Grant, c1805

I loved my Dad. I loved him when I didn't even know what the word meant. I used to get excited waiting for him to come home. I would see him coming or I'd hear the latch lift on the back door. Then I'd bury my head under his arm which smelled of flour and warm bread.

Ricky Tomlinson

Dad would bring the bathtub up on a Friday night and I had a bath in front of the fire. Friday night was also when the insurance man called. If he came while I was in the bath, Dad would push the tub, with me still in it, under the table and pull the cloth down. The insurance man would then be allowed into the house and only when he left would I be pulled out from under the table.

Patricia Cluderay

Dad hadn't a regular job, he just took what came along. In the summer, he dressed up in tails, top hat and spats, and carried a sandwich board advertising a café in the seaside town.

Another time he was a pirate on the *Hispaniola* sailing to 'Treasure Island' in the middle of the park lake. That, I think, was his favourite job.

One day he came swaggering down our street in his pirate costume, waving his sword in the air. When Mam opened the front door in answer to his loud knocking, she fell in a dead

Human beings are the only creatures that allow

faint as he waved his sword in front of her nose shouting "Yo ho ho and a bottle of rum, me hearties".

Nicholas Charles

Worldly rationalist though he was, or liked to think he was, my father had an eccentric side, which expressed itself every decade or so in a 'New Invention'. He spoke often of the 'genius' of the man who invented Cat's-eyes for night driving, and he aspired to a similarly grand scientific breakthrough.

Blake Morrison

My proudest moment when playing for Stainton came when Dad made a century and I was batting at the other end. I was nine years old, and again, was only playing because someone hadn't turned up. I can't recall my own score but that was of little consequence to me even then. The fact that I had been at the other end when Dad hit the runs that gave him a century was a tremendous thrill and a great source of pride.

Fred Trueman

I would have liked to take my parents to Lord's, to show them round, take them into the tavern and the Long Room. Dad would have loved that, but I never got the chance, I wish I had.

Geoffrey Boycott

My father suffered a heart attack and was ordered to bed. On that November evening a few days later, someone came to the door. "It's Mrs Hemingway." The figure of my parents' neighbour told me the worst. Two miles by bus and a quarter mile walk, carrying the news. Neighbourliness in action. I went back with her. My father was fifty-nine years old. I never stood at a bar counter and drank a beer with him. I have wished for many years that I could say otherwise.

Stan Barstow

their children to come back home. Bill Cosby

Our parents' cures for all ills were treacle and brimstone, and Parrishes Blood Mixture. My father once skinned a mouse, cleaned and roasted it, and my sister ate it as a cure for whooping cough, thinking it was a bird.

George A Jarratt

My mother Norah believed in plain home cooking — we couldn't afford anything else. Those were the days when chicken was a rare treat and, like lamb, was a traditional order from the butcher's shop at Eastertide.

Chickens were also bought at Christmas by mothers who could not afford the more exotic turkeys, and I will never forget the pride and excitement when my father arrived home with a goose. None of it was wasted, and goose grease was added to the family 'medicine chest'.

Goose grease was fatty, evil-smelling and rubbed into the skin, which glistened under the friction. It was reckoned to be a cure for ailments ranging from pneumonia, consumption, aching backs, rheumatism, pessimism and even Communism.

John Morgan

When my mother, Ethel, realised she was about to give birth, my father ran out of the house to bring the doctor. But I was fast even then. Speed coupled with a rhythmical approach and a good follow-through saw me into the world before my father had even reached the doctor's home.

Fred Trueman

I was their first child, and Mother had a hard time with the pregnancy. It made her even more sensitive than usual. For weeks she thought there was a funny smell in the kitchen. Dad finally had to take up the floorboards. "I couldn't find anything. Could I buggery."

Tom Courteney

It is easier for a father to have children than for

children to have a real father. Pope John XXIII

A wise mother will remove all traces of the day's toil before evening, as nothing upsets the rest of the family as much as leaving washing about the house. By evening the clothes are dried and ready for ironing, which may call for help from the elder girls of the family. If not, it is left for Tuesday morning. Our mother is then entitled to a 'sit down', but she is not idle, for there is always darning and mending to be done, the clogs making many holes in the stockings.

Oliver Greenwood

Piano

Softly, in the dusk, a woman is singing to me:
Taking me back down the vista of years, till I see
A child sitting under the piano, in the boom of the tingling strings
And pressing the small, poised feet of a mother who smiles
    as she sings.

In spite of myself, the insidious mastery of song
Betrays me back, till the heart of me sweeps to belong
To the old Sunday evenings at home, with winter outside
And hymns in the cosy parlour, the tinkling piano our guide.

So now it is vain for the singer to burst into clamour
With the great black piano appassionato. The glamour
Of childish days is upon me, my manhood is cast
Down in the flood of remembrance, I weep like a child for
    the past.

D H Lawrence

[My mother] was absolutely feminine, womanly, motherly ... I suppose I've got a mother complex. She was to me the absolute stability, the whole thing in life that one knew was there for one's protection. If she went out, I'd be terrified she wouldn't return. So it's not surprising that the kind of woman I've done in sculpture are mature women rather than young.

Henry Moore

I've been to war. I've raised twins. If I had a choice,

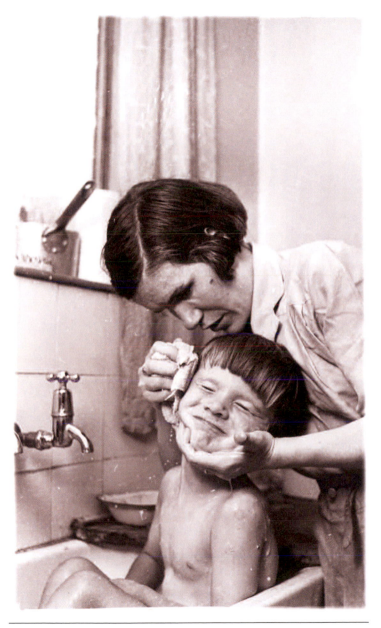

I'd rather go to war. George W Bush

Mother was always working. Most of the women went to the mill and did their housework afterwards. It was ten hours a day in the factory, rush home and prepare meals between, and then be at it every evening, washing, baking, cleaning, going to the town shopping on the Saturday half-day, and sometimes returning to do mending after that.

One evening during summer when I was seven, Mother called me in to go to bed. It was glorious outside and I wanted to go on playing, as children do on a bright and lovely evening, not realising in the late sunshine that it is past their usual bedtime. I resented going very much, and rebelled all the time I was washing and getting ready. As Mother tucked me in I questioned: "Why should anyone have to go to bed so early on a night like this?" Mother said she wished she could go to bed.

I realised why she said that, and felt sorry for her. I had seen her take off her clogs and heard her cry "Oh!" as she drew them from her puffed and swollen ankles and put on old shoes to ease her feet when she came home.

May Crew

I recall with pleasure the winter days when quilts were made to keep our beds warm during the bitterly cold nights. Were the winters more severe in those days or do I only remember them as such? At any rate, quilting days made a pleasant change when social events were few and far between.

Neighbours came to help with quilting; they obviously enjoyed the 'get-together' and the stitching was accompanied by much friendly chatter.

I kept one of mother's quilting templates for many years after her death because it symbolised a loving and resourceful woman whose chief aim in life was to ensure the comfort and well-being of her husband and family.

John Chippendale

Adam and Eve had many advantages, but the principal

Fragments of my parents' lives surface randomly: the 'demob' telegram from Kings Cross, stamped 'July 1945', that must have quickened the beat of my mother's heart; the honeymoon train journey to Blackpool by steam engine; a photo of them looking happy and relaxed strolling along the sea-front; two faded, pressed carnation sprays in the Bible; and a torn newspaper cutting of their wedding.

George Sweeting

A Parent's Prayer

Always believe in yourself.
Promise always to be compassionate.
Appreciate that you make mistakes,
Recognize that I do too.
Entrust me with your worries.
Never doubt that I will support you when you need me.
Talk to me about the things you find difficult.
Share your dreams.

Please understand that I can have moods just like you.
Receive a little advice now and again.
Accept that I sometimes get things wrong.
You need to help me to get things right.
Enjoy your life.
Realise that I lo ve you without reservation.

Gervase Phinn

one was that they escaped teething. Mark Twain

3. FAMILY AND FRIENDS

I have never felt in the shadow of my talented sister and brothers. I guess the fourth child in the family and the least able might have felt this, but I never did.

Christine, the eldest, passed her scholarship exam with flying colours to attend Notre Dame High School in Sheffield and went on to graduate with a fine degree and top-class teaching certificate. She became an art teacher, examiner and lecturer. I cannot count the number of times one of her former pupils has approached me over the years to tell me what an amazing teacher she was. I knew that already, for she had guided me through my GCE O- and A-Levels with incredible patience.

Michael my eldest brother, who owns a steelworks, can design anything, make anything and mend anything. At eighteen he had built his own sports car. He also has a fine voice.

When I approach a child, he inspires in me two sentiments; tenderness

Once at mass at St Bede's Church, Masborough, the soloist in the choir sang *Panis Angelicus* in a beautiful clear tenor voice. After the service Father Hammond, the parish priest, stood at the church door shaking hands with his parishioners.

"You must be very proud of your son, Mrs Phinn," he said.

"I am," said my mother, looking down and smiling at me.

"No," said the priest, "I meant your other son, Michael. It was he who was singing the solo part at this morning's mass."

My mother never recognised his voice.

Alec, my other brother, is, like my sister, a talented artist, and as a teenager he would spend hours sketching, drawing, painting delicate watercolours, producing the most vivid oil paintings. His other love was music, and he departed for Ireland where he now lives, a professional artist and musician.

So, I could have felt somewhat inadequate following in the line of such able and talented siblings, but I never did. My parents, like all great parents, made me feel very special, constantly stressing my own achievements, encouraging me to try my best and never ever comparing me unfavourably with my sister and brothers. I grew up with self-esteem and an expectation that I would do well in life, the two vital ingredients which help a child to succeed.

"Aim for the moon," my mother would say, "and one day you may go through the roof and dwell amongst the stars."

Gervase Phinn

———————

I think my Mam liked to think her family was a little bit more refined than the Tomlinsons. For one thing they lived in a slightly nicer street and had a parlour house with a proper hallway, rather than having a front door that opened directly into the 'best room'. Gran Wilson was also not the sort to get involved in knife fights at work.

Ricky Tomlinson

for what he is, and respect for what he may become. Louis Pasteur

Childhood

I used to think that grown-up people chose
To have stiff backs and wrinkles round their nose,
And veins like small fat snakes on either hand,
On purpose to be grand.
Till through the bannisters I watched one day
My great-aunt Etty's friend who was going away.
And how her onyx beads had come unstrung.
I saw her grope to find them as they rolled;
And then I knew that she was helplessly old,
As I was helplessly young.

Frances Cornford

There was an easy familiarity in our village, and the prefix 'Mr' would rarely be heard ... almost every man would be known, not as William Jones, but Bill o' Jack's, Joe o' Bob's, Tom o' Mary's. Many would be known by their trade or occupation. Such names as Tommy Joiner, Charley Fish, Joe Tinner, Tom Blacksmith, Tom Butcher, John Painter, Jack Clogger, Jack Mechanic, indicated at once who they were, and the recipients of these names took them for granted.

Nicholas Charles

I can locate the warm heart of my childhood in the big family parties that my grandparents held at Christmas. How many there were I can't now say, and perhaps one very successful one, with a score of more relatives crammed into the small cottage, has left its happiness like a stain on my memory ever since. In the roasting heat of two huge fires, the square table in one room would be laden with all the good things of high tea, and games in the other would reduce the womenfolk and the children to helpless laughter.

Stan Barstow

Before I got married I had six theories about bringing up children;

My Granddad

My granddad picked and chewed fresh hawthorn leaves,
Called it 'bread and cheese',
Smoked Bruno Flake,
Ate kippers, sucking clean each bone.

We children would dash, screaming, laughing,
Dodging a waving strap
Which he would wield at will
To entertain us.

Or, when we came in hungry from our play,
The bread he cut for us
So carefully upon the boiler-top
Seemed always thick and new.

My granddad met us little girls from school,
Waiting discreetly, almost out of sight,
Then from his pocket depths
He would present his gift —
The bag of sweets bought from the local market —
And follow us back home
At a convenient distance,
Puffing at his pipe.

He was a mild man — peace at any price,
Or nearly — as in later years
We were to know.
He died as he had lived.
Quite quietly.

Dora Berry

now I have six children and no theories. John Wilmot, Earl of Rochester

Grandpa Bain

I knew he could be fierce, and more than once
I heard him reprimand his grown-up sons,
my two indulgent uncles, and I'd sense —
although, behind his back, they'd wink and grin —
they dared not show defiance to his face.
I was aged nine; he never raised his voice
to me; it stayed a gently rumbling bass,
whatever kind of mood he might be in.

His right eye was a milky smear, quite blind;
the other eye, he told me, "wasn't grand",
though he could see enough to get around
but couldn't read the things that once he'd read.
And so I read to him the simple prose
and verse that I enjoyed, which seemed to please
him too. The knowing uncles smirked at us.
"Dad never was a scholar," Grandma said.

Vernon Scannell

I remember a crowd of flat-capped working men behind a
haze of Woodbine smoke at the town football ground in the
1950s. Protectively, Grandfather Tom used to usher us to the
touchline so that we could clearly see the match. Somehow,
this made me feel important.

George Sweeting

My younger brother Tony was a game little devil who took an
early fancy to a drop of the hard stuff, in his case the beer that
my granddad used to get in refillable bottles from the local
off-licence. Since Tony kept me in oranges, apples and broken
biscuits, the least I could do was help him out when we
visited Granddad. The beer bottle sat enticingly on the

Childhood: The period of human life intermediate between

the idiocy of infancy and the folly of youth. Ambrose Bierce

sideboard — my job was to keep Granddad occupied in conversation while Tony skilfully uncorked the bottle and had a swig. He became quite adept at it, and Granddad wasn't mobile enough to post a threat.

Geoffrey Boycott

I liked being near my grandmother. I was very fond of her and she favoured me. I quickly got into the habit of going to her for the little treats my mother sometimes chose to deny me: a bun or a piece of cake; a copper for sweets ('spice' in local parlance); sometimes the price of admission to the local cinema when my pocket money had run out.

In return for all my grandmother's treats, though none was needed, I taught this working-class wife of the Victorian age to write her name: Lydia Gosnay.

Stan Barstow

Grandma Quest was a typical Fish Dock worker's wife. She defended me stoutly when the little girl in Eton Street ratted on me for lifting up her skirt. "He only wants to see what's there," she said, and I was grateful for her support.

Tom Courtenay

On one awful occasion, I remember Grandma had to knock something off the visitor's bill to our family guest house in at the end of the week because I had ruined her son Arthur's best suit.

I had taken Arthur down to the harbour when the Scottish herring fleet was in. We had gloried in the smell of tar and the shouts of the sailors. With a crowd of other small boys, we raced the screaming gulls for the herrings that fell off the loaded lorries.

We set up rival stalls for our booty and scrawled notices on bits of packing paper: "Herrings, Penny Each". Arthur was

You know your children are growing up when they stop asking you where

drawing all the unsuspecting tourists to his stall. His herrings were advertised at "Two a Penny". This was shameful. Herrings had been one a penny ever since we could remember. Arthur came from Sheffield and must have had more of the business man about him than the fighting man. He was looking very sorry for himself by the time we'd finished with him.

Arthur returned to the bosom of his family an aggrieved and inured hero, and of course, it was all my fault.

Nicholas Charles

Our family had come a long way with our inside lavatory, but when I went to stay with my grandma in Halifax, I always hated the outside toilet. In winter, I'd pee in the snow, but that was always detected. So I took to constipating, but that's a crime in Yorkshire, treated with Andrew's Liver Salts, to which I long addicted, particularly mixed with sherbert.

Austin Mitchell MP

My girlfriend's grandmother had a yearning for Scarborough Spa Water — 6d a glass on the clifftop, or freely available on the prom below; she swore nothing helped her better. So for eight weekends in 1937 I picked up my girlfriend and, on our tandem, we rode the 100-odd miles to collect a gallon jar full. After a sometimes uneasy night at the YHA, the ride back taxed our energies and the tedious struggle made us doubt our mission; but grandma's appreciation left us in no doubt.

C Metcalfe

My most vivid memory of those days is of going up to bed at the end of the day. I always had to go up with Grandma. Whether it was her extreme age, or my extreme youth, that singled us out for this nightly pilgrimage together I never knew. Bedtime was half-past eight prompt. Grandma would heave herself slowly and painfully up the first of the three

---

they came from and refuse to tell you where they're going. P J O'Rourke

flights of stairs, hanging on to me with one hand and the banister with the other.

I soon became impatient of this snail's pace and would race to the first landing. There, on the table, were some celluloid tulips — salmon pink and gaudy yellow, on spring stalks. When I hit these they would quiver and spring back with a satisfying 'boing'. Grandma would negotiate the next flight even more slowly, muttering and wheezing sadly about the wickedness of boys. At the top of this flight, she sat down to rest on a dusty little carved chair.

Above us was all the horrible mystery of the top floor, where Grandma and I were banished for the season. Big mahogany wardrobes on the landing would sigh and groan in the middle of the night. A fiendish water cistern behind a frayed curtain would gurgle alarmingly. From our attic room, we could see the full glory of summer storms. I would lie stiff and trembling while the thunder rolled, and the bed was shaken with Grandma's snores.

Nicholas Charles

We visited my Gran fairly often. Though only twenty-odd miles away, it seemed an epic journey then. She was turned seventy when I was born and died at eighty-two in Coronation year. She was a hangover from a late Victorian working-class background. She'd had a hard life, living as a widow since 1926. She had been in service and did cleaning locally, laying out the dead and helping with births. She was not unkind but I don't recall much affection, and maybe that is a family trait.

Richard Riley

Grandma Quest once asked me if I knew the difference between little boys and little girls.

"What?" I asked, with a mixture of keen anticipation and acute embarrassment.

If your baby is beautiful and perfect, never cries or fusses, sleeps on

"Little boys have a tide mark just here," said Grandma, and she pulled back the sleeve of my jersey.

Sure enough, there it was; a ring of darkness just above my wrist. I was torn between pride in being so masculine and shame that my economic use of soap and water was now known to the world.

Tom Courtenay

Our neighbour Mrs Mullen cut a frail figure under the blue-and-white striped apron she wore in the style of a market butcher. She was an excellent cook. But her family of growing lads had the lion's share and major portions. She learned how to tighten the belt of her pinafore and do without. I remember her saying: "I had a walk round the table for dinner. And another one for my tea. It was enough for me."

Mrs Mullen pecked at left-overs. She was just one of the many thin and self-sacrificing ladies we had as neighbours in days of prewar unemployment, dole queues and austerity.

John Morgan

Nothing could be dispensed with. Everything had a family history. There was the Stradivarius violin, wrapped in a red silk handkerchief, and laid in a wooden case. It had been given to my paternal grandmother by an old uncle who had ended his life under her roof.

He was reputed to have travelled in France and Italy; to have lived a wandering, bachelor's life, and to have acquired the violin from some mysterious source.

I dreamed of the day when Christies would hear of it, and the family fortune would be made. By peering through the slits, one could read the name and the date inside. Alas, it proved to be an imitation, and finally went for a few shillings to a learner.

E M J Reid

schedule and burps on time — you're a grandma. Theresa Bloomingdale

Cricket was playing an increasingly important part in my life. I seemed to have aptitude for it and I certainly took enormous pleasure in it. Uncle Algy took me under his wing.

Algy was on to a good thing, though I didn't give it a thought at the time. He used to take me with him to Ackworth, where he was a seam bowler, paying my bus fare from Fitzwilliam and back, and making sure I got a sandwich and a piece of cake for my tea on match days. I used to knock up with the team and field for them in pre-match practice. I even learned to score.

After the game Algy would put on the most gorgeous cream gabardine suit and call in at the Boot and Shoe, all dolled up and Brylcreemed, and ready for a night out. I drank lemonade and ate crisps outside until the bus came, then I took Algy's bag and headed off home. The point was that Algy with no cricket bag to cramp his style was liberated and probably dangerous. All I knew was that I'd had a terrific day.

Geoffrey Boycott

Uncle Stow was a case, he was. He was always laughing. You've never seen such a happy man. When he was five, he stowed away in his father's trawler and went to sea — so he was nicknamed 'Stow'.

Stow wouldn't go to school after his mother died and my mother kept telling him, if he didn't go, the policeman would come and take him away. One day he came running in and shut himself in the bedroom, crying "Don't let them take me away".

There was a policeman after him at the door.

My mother said: "What's he done? He's frightened to death — what's he done?"

"He's just saved a child from out of the harbour."

Stow thought the policeman was going to take him away because he hadn't been to school.

Mary Jane Dryden

I wish you would moderate that fondness you

My brothers were always at loggerheads with the town boys and would often fight them. On one occasion on going with my mother to see my aunt, the front door was spattered with blood, whether from the butcher boy's nose or the meat he'd thrown in self-defence I never found out.

Elizabeth Collingwood

When Mam and Grandma and Aunties were sitting at the table, drinking endless cups of tea, I used to play with my soldiers on the hearth-rug. Among the legs of the grown-ups, thick like tree-trunks, my imaginary battles would rage. Above my head flowed the talk — illnesses, operations, confinements. I took no notice of these conversations until the voices dropped to piercing, confidential whispers. Then I pricked up my ears.

Nicholas Charles

Auntie Maud was a kindly soul who had the gift of making children feel special and personally welcome, and was possessive to a point of greeting me with a hug and the delighted cry: "It's our John!" It made me feel wanted. I was not 'yours' but 'ours'. She always wore a floral pinafore, and when she pulled your shining little face on to her 'pinny', you enjoyed being suffocated with love and a feeling of complete and utter security.

John Morgan

We stayed with an aunt while mum was in hospital. Sweets were rationed but mum sent me a ½lb box of Black Magic for my birthday. It was very small with perhaps only six chocolates, but I was normally allowed to eat them before breakfast with a cup of tea in bed. My aunt brought them for me to open. She allowed me to have one and, even though I explained the routine, that was all before they were removed. I swear to this day that I never saw the rest of them again.

Richard Riley

have for your children. Mary Wortley Montagu

There was Adelaide, known as Addie, a jolly lady and nice to have for a great-aunt. Like her bulky sisters, Addie was not avoirdupois-deprived; indeed she was immensely proportioned, with a one-piece bosom which was a cross between a French provincial hotel bolster and a sandbag. In the garden she would lie back in her deckchair and park her cup of tea on nature's shelf; no hands.

Frank Muir

Aunt Eliza never went to the air-raid shelter without dressing to the nines. She put on her best coat, feather boa, Ascot-type hat, and gripped her favourite leather handbag, containing rosary beads, insurance policies and so on, and walked as stately as royalty to the shelter. When asked why she always put on her finery, Aunt Eliza answered: "If I am going to meet my maker, I want to be dressed for the occasion."

John Morgan

My sister had several boyfriends. She would offer me a penny if I would go on the pier with her. I don't know whether my father knew or approved of these friends. He probably thought she was taking me for a walk. Anyway, I went quite willingly, as to go on the pier cost money. In addition to my fee of a penny, my half fare on to the pier had to be paid as well. When we got to the end of the pier I was dismissed until it was time to return.

Elizabeth Collingwood

My cousin Lynda and I were bridesmaids for our mothers' cousin in February 1951 when Lynda was four and I was two. We wore crinoline dresses in lilac-coloured taffeta and net, with matching bonnets and pale green velvet capes. Because Lynda was older, I was told to hold her hand and not let go. Once inside the church, however, the vicar wanted to separate

Let us put our minds together and see what life

us. When I refused, he lost his temper and demanded that I was removed from the church. I spent the rest of the ceremony sitting in the church porch with my granddad, eating toffee — much more enjoyable.

Hazel Martell

A lot of people married their cousins. You never went further than the town because there was no need. Anyway you couldn't get outside. As you didn't go outside, they did inter-marry. Them that had twenty-one children were cousins. My father's sister married my mother's cousin and they had one boy. He looked the image of my father.

Mary Jane Dryden

we can make for our children. Sitting Bull

4. SCHOOLDAYS

I am five. The photograph shows a chubby little boy with a round pale face, a mop of black hair and large eyes, sitting on the back step of the house in Richard Road, taken just before he sets off for his first day at school. I am wearing a crisp white shirt and little tartan clip-on tie, short trousers which I eventually grow into, socks pulled up to the dimpled knees and large polished black shoes. I do not look at all happy. In fact, I seem in the verge of tears.

Broom Valley Infant School appeared to a small boy of five as a vast, cold and frightening castle of a building with its huge square metal-framed windows and endless echoey corridors, shiny green tiles, hard wooden floors, and the oppressive smell of stale cabbage and floor polish.

It was a daunting place, and on my first day — so my mother told me years later when my own children started school — I screamed and shouted, tugged and writhed as she held my small hand firmly in hers on our way to the entrance. I hated it, and wanted to go home and sit at the table in the kitchen and help my mother make gingerbread men and listen to her stories. When I saw her head for the door I thought I would be abandoned forever and couldn't be consoled.

"I want to go home!" I cried. "I want to go home!"

But I was made to stay and I spent the whole morning whimpering in a corner, resisting the kind attentions of Miss Greenhalgh, the infant teacher.

At morning playtime I couldn't be coaxed to eat the biscuit or drink the milk on offer, and continued to sniffle and whimper. But by lunchtime I had become intrigued and soon dried

A child of five would understand this. Send someone

my tears. Just before lunch Miss Greenhalgh opened a large coloured picture book and began to read. I loved books, and the bedtime routine was my mother or father or sister snuggling up with me to read. I knew all the nursery rhymes and the fairy stories and, although I couldn't read, I knew if a word was changed or a bit missed out, and would tell the reader so.

When Miss Greenhalgh opened the book on that first morning, I stopped the sniffling and listened. She looked to me like someone out of the pages of a fairy tale: long golden hair like Rapunzel's, large blue eyes like Snow White's, and such a gentle voice and lovely smile like Sleeping Beauty's. When she started reading the story, I was completely captivated.

The following morning I wolfed down my breakfast, keen to get back to school and Miss Greenhalgh.

Gervase Phinn

Notwithstanding the meanness [ie poverty] of ... my Parents, it pleased God to put it into their Hearts to put me to School, to learn both to read and write.

John Bunyan

About Five Years Old, I was put to School but being addicted to play, after the Example of my young School-fellows, I scarcely learnt to distinguish my Letters, before I was taken away to Work for my Living.

Thomas Tryon, c1700

My first day at school was very traumatic. I had never been away from home before. There were no playgroups or nursery schools then — you just went straight to school aged five. I remember coming home at lunchtime and being most put out when I found out I had to go back again.

Pauline Molineaux

to fetch me a child of five. Groucho Marx

I started school in September 1952 at the age of four, and my clearest memory is of the little canvas beds which were put up every afternoon for us to have a sleep. It was something I didn't do at home — and I didn't want to do it at school, either. Bored, I started waking the other children up to play with me. After I'd done this a few times and made some of them cry, the teacher allowed me to take a toy or a book from home and amuse myself so the others could sleep in peace.

Hazel Martell

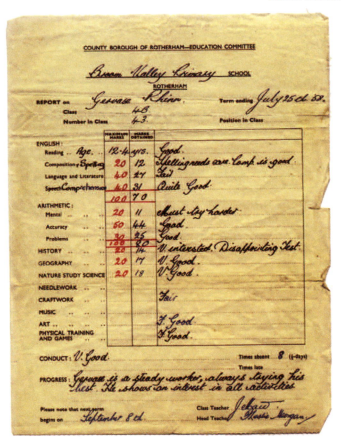

I must study politics and war that my sons may have liberty

On my first day at the new school, when I got in the class-room, the headmistress was sitting at her desk reading a daily newspaper.

"Well children, what's going to win today?" she asks.

I'd no idea what she was on about until one boy told her which horse he thought was a winner.

Norene Walbridge

School was almost two miles from my father's house, a great way for a little fat short-legged lad (as I was) to travel twice a day.

Adam Martindale, 1630

Think what you would have been now, if instead of being fed with Tales and Old Wives' Fables in childhood, you had been crammed with Geography and Natural History? Damn them. I mean the cursed Barbauld Crew, those Blights and Blasts of all that is Human in man and child.

Charles Lamb, letter to Coleridge, 1802

I was popular with my teachers — on Saturdays and Sundays.

Eric Morecambe

A friend who was put to work on the Burma railway once told me that he was greeted, on arrival, by a fellow prisoner-of-war who said: "Cheer up. It's not half as bad as Marlborough".

John Mortimer

If public school had taught me anything it was just generally to shoulder your way to the front when you wanted to. I begin to see now more of what I was then and why I'm like I am now. The relationships with people, which are quite hard to establish. I don't have vast numbers of friends. That's proba-bly all from a quite lonely childhood.

Alan Ayckbourn

---

to study mathematics and philosophy. John Adams

I had been made a prefect at school a year earlier than usual, and I had a nervous breakdown and was expelled. It was the responsibility, I think.

anon

I was sent by my mother to an old school-dame who lived at the very next door ... But I suppose I did continue here but a few days, for growing weary of my book, and my dame not correcting me as my mother desired, she took me under her pedagogy until I could read my Bible, and thus she did afterwards by all my brothers and sisters.

James Fretwell, c1710

I found an awful stench in school all week. Could not account for it till this morning, when I found it proceeded from a boy whose breath was so offensive as to cause an unpleasant odour to pervade the whole room. He went home at playtime. I told him to tell his mother to take him to the doctor.

schoolmaster's report, Yorkshire Dales, 1880s

Give me the children until they are seven and anyone

When he can talk 'tis time he should begin to learn to read, but as to this give me leave here to inculcate again what is very apt to be forgotten, namely that great care is to be taken that it be never made as a business to him nor he look upon it as a task. Their being forced and tied down to their books in an age at enmity with all such restraint has I doubt not been reason why a great many have hated books and learning all their lives after. It is like a surfeit which leaves an aversion behind not to be removed. Thus much for learning to read, which let him never be driven to nor chid for; cheat him into it if you can, but make it not a business for him. 'Tis better it be a year later before he can read than that he should this way get an aversion to learning. Lay no task on him about ABC. Use your skill to make his will supple and pliant to reason. Teach him to love credit and commendation, to abhor being thought ill or meanly of, especially by you and his mother, and then the rest will come all easily.

When by these easy ways he begins to read, some easy pleasant book suited to his capacity should be put into his hands wherein the entertainment that he find might draw him on and reward his pains in reading.

John Locke, 'Some Thoughts Concerning Education', 1693

Our uniforms were very uncomfortable, especially the knickers. We had to wear big bloomer-type things. Perhaps that's why I don't wear knickers now.

Vivienne Westwood

I wasn't just hopeless in class — I was terrible.

Eric Morecambe

He has glaring faults and they have certainly glared at us this term.

Stephen Fry, school report, Uppingham School

may have them afterwards. St Francis Xavier

It's true that some Gypsy girls are brought up to cook and clean the house and get married, and some boys are brought up to go round collecting scrap metal to bring money into the home, but I was brought up to believe that I could do anything I want to do. Neither my dad nor my uncles can read or write, and all my family are very proud of what I've achieved at school.

Dean Vine

No matter what his rank or position may be, the lover of books is the

In 1899 the first scholars, a boy and girl, went to Skipton to sit the county examination for admission to the local grammar schools. The girl travelled in a pony trap, but unfortunately the pony had a fright on the way, kicked the front of the trap to pieces and tipped the girl out — a poor preliminary for an examination. The boy, having no other means of transport, went and returned by coal wagon, the journey taking four hours each way.

S E Raistrick

None of my family went to grammar school because you had to pay. You had to pass a scholarship examination. My brother passed and I passed; I suppose we were unusual. I knew I couldn't go because there was no one to pay for my books.

Mary Jane Dryden

My stay in hospital came at an unfortunate time. Members of my class in school were being prepared for the county minor scholarship examination and a place at grammar school. Most children at that time left school at fourteen and found what jobs they could. The minority who transferred to grammar school at eleven had a stepping stone to university, or at least a chance of something other than manual or semi-skilled employment. The time I'd had off school was now thought to have jeopardised my chances. All the same, I passed. The results must have been read out Monday morning assembly because I clearly recall hurtling out of school at midday and running all the way up Cluntergate to burst into a house full of steam, where my mother and my grandmother were standing over a peggy tub full of washing.

"I've passed! I've passed!" I told them.

And though I must confess that I passed little else afterwards, I cannot disparage that achievement.

Stan Barstow

richest and the happiest of the children of men. John Alfred Langford

Children make the most desirable opponents in Scrabble as

I was put in for the scholarship. I remember the rating I got because I didn't pass. I was fully expected to pass, but I didn't try because I knew that if I passed, I couldn't go. I wanted to pass, but you see it was no use, because although there was help, it wouldn't have been enough for our family.

Actually, I didn't try and I was hauled over the coals. The headmistress had me in, didn't she? "Why didn't you pass? What did you do?" And I suppose I didn't answer. "I don't know," I said ...

I would have liked to have been a teacher but, you see, I knew what I was going to do and it was something I wasn't going to like.

I had to go into service [at fourteen], for one thing to make room for the boys to sleep as they got older.

Jane Taverner

I told my father I failed to get to secondary school because he made me have violin lessons three nights a week, which cost a shilling a night. I hated the noise I made. So I said: "Dad, you know why I failed, I haven't done the homework because three nights a week you made me do the violin."

Henry Moore

Mam and Dad must have been both puzzled and worried by my wanting to go on the stage. Where had such an absurd not-ing come from? (Where indeed?)

They had always been aware of their own lack of education, and therefore of opportunity, and they believed that I would be better equipped to make my way in the world if I went to a university. My getting a good education was very important to them.

Nobody from West Dock Avenue School had ever been to a university. I was the first, and I think the last.

Tom Courtenay

they are easy to beat and fun to cheat. Fran Lebowitz

We were the subjects of a far more important hierarchy than that headed by king and parliament.

Our leaders were Bertha Lonsdale in the library, looked upon with awe because she did stories for the BBC; Father Archer the vicar, whom we Methodists viewed with distaste because he'd been seen in the Bay Horse; and Alec Clegg, the West Riding's director of education, whose children we were. He was God for me. When I was a boy, he appeared to take personally all the decisions affecting our lives, which were mostly to keep scholarship kids like me moving upwards and out, away from our roots and mates.

As a result of this benevolence, we ended up not really part of anything; neither where we came from, nor where we were being siphoned to.

Austin Mitchell MP

I must have been eleven or twelve, and things were so tight that mother had to apply for me to have meals at school, which if people were very poor, they could have free. I remember the humiliation I felt, going to school to have breakfast. It consisted of two pieces of bread and jam and a cup of cocoa, and the dinner was always a stew of some kind. But I can feel now the humiliation, all of my school friends knowing that my mother was too poor to feed me.

Edith Smith, c1910

The School Meals Service endeavours to move with the times, educating the children to try new foods. The cooks themselves are encouraged to branch out and use new recipes, so that meals are interesting and not just 'meat and two veg' followed by pudding.

While not pandering to faddy tastes, it is wasteful to serve particular types of food, which get left. Sometimes, like mothers, the cooks disguise such foods, by serving in a

What a distressing contrast there is between the radiant intelligence of

the child and the feeble mentality of the average adult. Sigmund Freud

How is it that little children are so intelligent and men so

different manner, calling them by a fancy name, or adding an interesting sauce.

In Le Cateau Junior School, there is kitchen staff of five and one server. About 160 children, mainly from the Services, are catered for, and it has been discovered that due to their much-travelled lives there is a great liking for spiced and highly seasoned foods. Sauces and curried dishes, which may not be so popular at other schools, are eaten here with relish.

Joan Walkland, 1962

A tuck-box is a small pinewood trunk which is very strongly made, and no boy has ever gone as a boarder to an English prep school without one. It is his own secret store-house, as secret as a lady's handbag, and there is an unwritten law that no other boy, no teacher, not even the headmaster himself has the right to pry into the contents of your tuck-box.

As well as tuck, a tuck-box would also contain all manner of treasures such as a magnet, a pocket-knife, a compass, a ball of string, a clockwork racing-car, half a dozen lead soldiers, a box of conjuring tricks, some tiddly-winks, a Mexican jumping bean, a catapult, some foreign stamps, a couple of stink-bombs, and I remember one boy called Arkle who drilled an airhole in the lid of his tuck-box and kept a pet frog in there which he fed on slugs.

Roald Dahl

He has no ambition.

Sir Winston Churchill, school report, Ascot School

When I was about seven years of age, I remember I had one time eight tutors in several qualities, languages, music, dancing, writing, and needlework, but my genius was quite averse from all but my book, and that I was so eager of, that my mother thinking it prejudiced my health, would moderate me

stupid? It must be education that does it. Alexandre Dumas

in it; yet this rather animated me than kept me back, and every moment I could steal from my play I would employ in any book I could find, when my own were locked up from me.

After dinner and supper I still had an hour allowed me to play, and then I would steal into some hole or other to read. My father would have me learn Latin, and I was so apt that I outstripped my brothers who were at school...

My brothers who had a great deal of wit, had some emulation at the progress I made in my learning, which very well pleased my father, though my mother would have been contented, I had not so wholly addicted myself to that as to neglect my other qualities; as for music and dancing I profited very little in them and would never practise my lute or harpsichords but when my sisters were with me; and for my needle I absolutely hated it.

Lucy Apsley, 1627

Judi would be a very good pupil if she lived in this world.

Dame Judi Dench OBE, school report

All this while, tho' now about Thirteen Years Old, I could not Read: then thinking of the vast usefulness of Reading, I bought me a Primer, and got now one, then another, to teach me to Spell, and so learn'd to Read imperfectly, my Teachers themselves not being ready Readers; But in a little time having learn't to Read competently well, I was desirous to learn to Write, but was at a great loss for a Master, none of my Fellow-Shepherds being able to teach me. At last, I bethought myself of a lame young Man who taught some poor People's Children to Read and Write; and having by this time got two Sheep of my own, I applied to him, and agreed with him to give him one of my Sheep to teach me to make the Letters, and joyn them together.

Thomas Tryon, c1700

Children pick up words as pigeons pick up peas,

And utter them again as the good God shall please. English proverb

Village School

The little village school has closed,
The gate is shut, the rooms are bare;
The desks where children worked or dozed
Are empty, dust is lying there.

If stones would speak, and walls could tell,
Of youth they sheltered day by day
From spring to winter, bell to bell,
What tales we'd hear of work and play.

For all the hopes, desires and joys
Of village life were centred there,
The apple-cheeked, the girls, the boys,
Came in procession year by year.

The grandfathers, and then the sons —
Who grew, and left to work the land,
The daughters, and their little ones,
All came, once shy, and hand in hand.

The whistle blew, the playground rang
With shouts; inside the rooms were bright,
Where sums were learned and scholars sang
And teachers taught of wrong and right.

Progress is such that people choose
To sweep the small into its tide —
In gaining more how much we lose
Of value in our countryside.

Long may the village schools that thrive
Remain, an English heritage
For village children — warm, alive,
Not symbols of a passing age.

Margaret G Jones

Children are remarkable for their intelligence, for their curiosity, their

intolerance of shams, the clarity and ruthlessness of their vision. Aldous Huxley

The schoolmaster had wide country interests — fishing, gardening, natural history — and knew how to make use of unexpected opportunities. A boy killed a rabbit on the way to school, so there was a lesson on the rabbit; a 'Spider' followed the discovery of a spider's cocoon in the moss on the wall of the school playground. A thrush built a nest in the ivy on the wall and a house-martin in the boys' porch, so 'Birds and their Nests' was the lesson; a boy brought a dead mole to school on one occasion and a dead water-rat on another, so a lesson on 'Moles and Vole' was given, followed by a demonstration of skinning and curing the skins.

S E Raistrick

A Child of the Dales

From the classroom window rolled the great expanse of the Dale.
The sad child in the corner stared out like a rabbit in a trap.
"He has special needs," explained the teacher, in a hushed,
   maternal voice.
"Real problems with his reading, and his number work is weak.
Spelling non-existent, writing poor. He rarely speaks.
He's one of the less able in the school."

The lad could not describe the beauty that surrounded him,
The soft green dale and craggy hills.
He could not spell the names
Of those mysterious places which he knew so well.
But he could tickle a trout, ride a horse,
Repair a fence and dig a dyke,
Drive a tractor, plough a field,
Milk a cow and lamb a ewe,
Name a bird by a faded feather,
Smell the seasons and predict the weather.
Yes, that less able child could do all those things.

Gervase Phinn

Grown men can learn from very little children for

From the age of ten or twelve years, we were very much taken off the Schoole, espetialy in the spring and summer season, plow time, turfe time, hay time and harvest, in looking after the sheep, helping at plough, goeing to the moss with carts, making hay and shearing in harvest, two of us at 13 or 14 years of age being equall to one man shearer; so that we made small progress in Latin, for what we got in winter we forgot in summer, and the writing master coming to Boulton mostly in winter, wee got what writing we had in winter.

William Stout, 1675

At country schools, your masters drive you on by fear.

Richard Baxter, c1670

It became apparent, even to the pupils, that the school wasn't actually surviving. By the last couple of terms the headmaster and his wife were keeping it open for about six of us who had to sit our Common Entrance exams. We were like family by then. Most of the place was just closed up. The gymnasium had become pigsties. They'd turned it into a farm, and I used to spend days and weeks with a scythe just clearing hedges and ditches, acres of brambles and stinging nettles. Very cheap labour ... I loved doing it. I think they ploughed up the cricket pitch.

Alan Ayckbourn

There were games of conkers, marbles under the tree in the schoolyard, and ladybird and grasshopper races.

John Iveson

Boys from the schools bring fighting cocks to their master, and the whole forenoon is given up to boyish sport; for they have a holiday in the schools that they may watch their cocks do battle.

William FitzStephen, describing twelfth-century London

the hearts of little children are pure. Black Elk

I spent most of my time in the school lavatory smoking anything I could ignite.

Eric Morecambe

I was a born gazer-out-of-the-windows. Grinding shops, cutlery in its rough stages, waterwheels, mill dams, sluices, tiddlers — to me as a child, industry was just life, interesting and colourful.

Arthur Kitching

I never knew how many apples a farmer had left in his basket if he gave his wife two-thirds. Or how much water slipped away in an hour if the bath-plug was released and the tap dripped at the rate of fifty drops per minute. What the Hell! I was lost.

Dirk Bogarde

The lighthouse station was controlled by Hull Trinity House, who would not provide a school and teacher for us, which caused five families to leave Spurn Point together. The ages of the children ranged up to twelve years, and we left Spurn ignorant of school learning and nervous of having to mix with people and children much more advanced in everything than we were.

George A Jarratt

There were four classes in our classroom. Keeping order and instructing us all was Daddy Hunt. He was a tyrant but perhaps he needed to be to keep such a motley crew of boys and girls in order.

Heads down at our books, but suddenly heads were raised and the whisper went round: "Jack Dunn is baking potatoes".

Playtime couldn't come too soon, and then it was over to Jack's with a handkerchief and one penny. They were still in their skins but tasted lovely.

Geoff Townsend

It is no less true in the human kingdom of knowledge, that no man shall

enter into it 'except that he becomes first as a little child'. Valerius Terminus

My education, such as it was, was like that of thousands in my day. I went to old Betty W's School, and as I had 'finished my education' when I was seven years old, I must have attended her school between three or four years.

The school was the only room on the ground floor of her little cottage ... The furniture was very scant, consisting of a small table, two chairs, and two or three little forms about eight inches high for the children to sit upon...

There was an alphabet, with rude pictures, for beginners. There must have been something intensely vivid about these letters in the alphabet, for to this day when I see the letter Q and S as single capitals I see them rather as when I first saw them in old Betty's alphabet...

Betty's next grade, after the alphabet, was the reading-made-easy book, with black letters, making words in two, three and four letters.

The next stage was spelling, and reading of the Bible. Though she never taught writing, her scholars were generally noted for their ability to read while very young. I know I could read my Bible with remarkable ease when I left her school, when seven years old.

Charles Shaw, 1840

I never remarked on so irreconcilable and implacable a spirit as that of Boyes against their Schoolmasters or Tutors. The quarrels of their Education have an influence upon their Memories and Understandings for ever after. They cannot speak of their Teachers with any patience or civility: and their discourse is never so flippant, nor their Wits so fluent, as when you put them upon that 'Theme'.

Andrew Marvell

The affairs are ill-managed by a committee of languid, educationally inept amateurs, and the school is staffed by

Large streams from little fountains flow:

incompetent and unscrupulous teachers. To form the minds of children and direct their powers of reading into beneficial channels, the teacher must know much more than is expressed in the lessons themselves.

The head teacher is so absorbed in administrative and financial duties that he underrates the functions connected with the intellectual management of the school.

From 'The Inspector's Report to the School Board', 1854

Attention is drawn to the following directives which the staff of the establishment might well apply:
- To promote, by precept and example, cleanliness, neatness and decency;
- To impress a time and a place for everything and everything in its proper place;
- To treat pupils with kindness and firmness;
- To keep a register, report book and class lists accurately and neatly;
- To teach to the Board's school books

Practical Rules for Teachers, 1844

We had a French and a German mistress, and were supposed to speak one or other of these languages. We spoke English when the headmistress was out of the schoolroom, harassing and annoying these unfortunate women. I can see even now the German woman's black eyes, the heavy pallid face as she spat, no doubt well-deserved, epithets at us in German.

Elizabeth Collingwood

On returning to my first school, I was told it was my turn to do my 'piece' or 'turn'. One could, sing, recite, make something or whatever.

Being shy to the point of stupid I panicked, too scared to make a run for it. I picked up the chalk and went to the

Tall oaks from little acorns grow. David Everett

blackboard. I wrote 'How to make elderberry wine' and a list of ingredients.

After I'd finished, the class had to ask questions, one of which was "Does it make you drunk?" "Rephrase that," called the teacher. "'Does it make you intoxicated?'"

Norene Walbridge

The teaching we were exposed to was offered on a kind of take-it-or-leave-it basis. It was tossed to you and what you didn't catch you lost. Bad luck played its part. The girl I would marry was enthused in her English by the teaching of Mavis 'Salomé' Mercer; I had my own interest dampened by the dullest master in the school, whose idea of analysing *Macbeth* and bringing it to life for us was to fill the blackboard with endless notes for us to copy.

Stan Barstow

The most fascinating teacher at Kingston High School was Mr Large, the senior English master. He was slim and dark, with piercing brown eyes and a far more histrionic manner than any of the others. He produced the school play every year before Christmas. It was cast from the sixth form only; but I was determined to let Mr Large know of my existence as soon as I possibly could.

Tom Courtenay

Away from the classroom, however, I'd begun to play — and fall in love with — cricket. I clearly remember one day hearing Miss Nelson through the partition reprimanding one of the seniors for his lacklustre attitude during a school cricket match.

"Go and watch young Freddie Trueman play cricket if you want to know what determination and the right attitude is all about," I heard her say.

When a child asks you something, answer him, for goodness'

I was taken aback. It was the first time anyone had passed favourable comment about my ability as a cricketer, and I also felt a sense of pride in being cited as a good example to someone older than me.

Fred Trueman

My primary school teacher used to say to me that I was going to be either a singer or a writer. She was quite right. These are the two things that I felt I wanted to do. When she was teaching the class a song, she knew that I would learn it in about two minutes flat, so then she made me sing it to the rest of the class. I remember that that lady had great faith in me from a very early age.

Janet Barber

I could read before I went to infants' school, but when the unpleasant headmistress asked me to read from the board, I couldn't, so she wrote me off as a liar and a dunce. The young reception-class teacher Miss Appleton didn't agree. At playtime she asked me to read from a book, which I did. She then wrote something on the board and I was dumbstruck. The following week I had an eye test, glasses were duly issued and all was well. I owe a lot to that perceptive young woman.

Mavis Holt

Schooldays are supposed to be the happiest days of our lives. None of us is aware of it at the time, of course, and I suppose that as a schoolboy I was very much like any other — sometimes worried by the thought of the next, unfathomable lesson, sometimes totally oblivious, always in and out of trouble. We were fortunate in that we had masters of outstanding quality who took a real interest in what we did — and in some cases still do.

Geoffrey Boycott

sake. But don't make a production of it. Harper Lee

He shows great originality, which must be curbed at all costs.

Sir Peter Ustinov CBE, school report, Westminster School

I loved painting, but the painting master was a thoroughly nasty old man. He rubbed his old cheek against the faces of the girls he liked. I hated being pawed by him.

Elizabeth Collingwood

The person who made the most difference to my future career as a teacher was my aunt. I recounted to her a school visit to a large cotton mill and my horror at the deafening, clanking noise of the looms, and the tired-looking girls who manned them. "Well, that's where you'll be, my girl, if you don't do more homework, and pass the scholarship to the grammar school," she said. I worked in fear of my fate, and duly passed.

Ruth Newey

The teacher would either smack me in front of the class or send me off to be caned. Whatever he hoped to achieve by such public ridicule I do not know, but its effect was to turn me against the school and all it stood for, and to alienate me from my classmates.

Ernie Wise

A talkative pupil had to wear his gas mask for the whole day to shut him up.

John Iveson

The boy is every inch a fool but luckily for him he's not very tall. Although I doubt any possibility of his ever being promoted, he may get sufficient marks to obtain his proficiency pay, and who knows, with a little bit of luck, he may perhaps, in time — about twenty-one years — get a pension.

Sir Norman Wisdom OBE, Army Education exam report

A young child is, indeed, a true scientist, just one big

question mark. What? Why? How? Victoria Wagner

Remembering Mr Firth

So,
You are curious to know
What sort of man he was,
What kind of teacher.
Some, I guess, would say that he was unpredictable and loud
Heavy-handed, hard-headed, proud,
A fiery figure with his froth of wild white hair
And bright all-seeing eyes,
That he talked too much
And listened too little.

Well,
I'll tell you.
He was a teacher
Who lifted dreary history from the dusty page,
Refought bloody battles on a chalky board.
A storyteller who painted pictures of the past in vivid colour,
An enthusiast, who with bursts of energy
And eyes gleaming with a quick impassioned fire,
Resurrected shadowy characters of a bygone age:
Fabled kings and tragic queens, pale-faced martyrs and
    holy monks,
Princes and peasants, tyrants and warriors.
He bought history to life.

I recall,
One cold November day
In a hushed classroom
When he told the story of the sorrowful Scottish Queen
Who climbed the scaffold stiffly,
Clad in a gown the colour of dried blood,
To meet her fate at Fotheringhay
And we felt that we were there.

Gervase Phinn

Too often we give our children answers to remember

The cane was a deterrent, but not for those who discovered a stone with magical properties. It was a glassy, smooth rock known as 'cane-snap', and we believed that if you rubbed it on your palms the cane would break on impact. I was nominated our school's first guinea pig. I was summoned for a whacking, but I winked with glee at those sharing deep confidence in 'cane-snap'. Two searing stripes across each hand quickly dispelled that conviction. I almost hit the ceiling and the weals were visible for a couple of hours. I am afraid the 'cane-snap' did not work for me or anyone else.

John Morgan

The archaic form of punishment was to be given an 'entry' in the teacher's book for some alleged misconduct. After three pencil entries you would have an ink entry, which was getting serious, and after three such entries, which could have been accumulated for nothing more than chatting in class, you would be thrashed with a cane by the PT master.

I was the first in the class to suffer this humiliation. The stripes became quite severe weals on my backside.

Mum was shocked but thought it was something to do with grammar-school discipline. You accepted your punishment, since you always did what you were told.

Steven Berkoff

Constantly late for school, losing his books and papers and various other things into which I need not enter. He is so regular in his irregularity that I really don't know what to do. He had such good abilities but these would be "made useless by habitual negligence".

Sir Winston Churchill, school report, Harrow School

On second thoughts I can't say that my school days were the happiest days of my life. Up to the age of about seven I was

rather than problems to solve. Roger Lewin

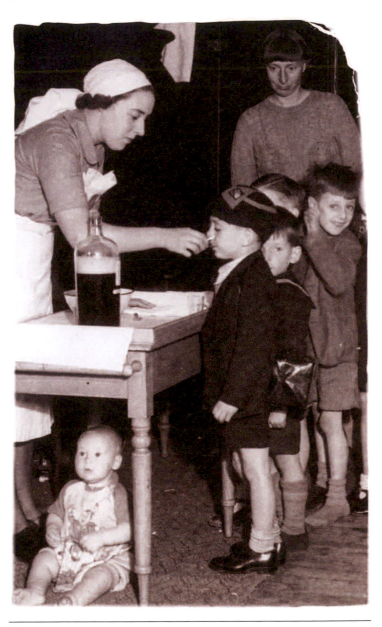

All children are artists. The problem is how to remain

happy enough. Then something happened to 'upset the apple cart,' as they used to say. The something was Miss Bigley.

Whenever I look back to my school days I see her — a large, mannish woman, in a black dress. As well as a small gold watch worn on her dress, she had an unsightly ridge, which clearly defined the tops of her stays.

What Miss Bigley taught me was almost entirely about myself. She said I was a day-dreamer; I talked too much; and I was deaf; I was inattentive and unpunctual; also I asked to leave the room too many times.

When we marched in the playground she said I didn't know my right wheel from my left wheel. I did really, but being a bit on the nervous side, I did all the wrong things in trying to please my teacher, like putting up my hand when I'd no answer to give.

After all, with about sixty-odd other children to teach, Miss Bigley couldn't be blamed for losing her patience with me.

William Taylor

I remember we all tried to show the girls how tough we were when the school dentist came with his foot-operated pedal drill. He used to 'operate' at Mrs Wood's so our howls of pain could not be heard at school.

John Iveson

And when [my governess] did see me idly disposed she wod sett me to cipher with my pen, and to cast up and prove great sums and accompts, and sometimes to wryte a supposed letter to this or that body concerning such and such things, and other tymes let me read in *Dr Turner's Herball* and *Bartholomew Vigoe*, and at other tymes sett me to sing psalms, and other tymes sett me to soe curious work; for she was an excellent woman in all kinds of needlework.

Grace Sherrington, c1560

an artist once he grows up. Pablo Picasso

The one bit of encouragement I got concerning my longed-for career came from a comparative outsider.

Mr Stannard, the art master, was away ill, and the teacher who took his place for a few weeks saw me reading the lessons in prayer one morning. I had to call in the art room and he was sitting at his desk surrounded by several sixth-form girls.

"You were terrific in assembly this morning, I've never seen such a young lad so at home on a stage. You should become an actor."

The girls' proximity made his remarks all the more magical.

"Thank you, sir, but everybody says you can't make a living as an actor."

"I have a friend at Liverpool Rep who earns £20 a week. If that's what you want to do, don't let anybody put you off."

His words were so unexpected and so much what I wanted to hear that they took my breath away.

Tom Courtenay

Don't get panarchy
I don't want anarchy,
Just sympathy
For the pimply.

anon

Some people you never forget in life. Your first love. Your driving instructor. The person who was always top of the class. The couple who never returned the invitation to your party. Likewise there are some things we never forget. The multiplication tables for example, that I was taught parrot-fashion at school. To this day should anyone ask me my multiplication from any table from one to twelve I answer in an instant.

Fred Trueman

I believe that it is better to restrain children by feelings

of shame, and by kindness, than by fear. Terence

As a child I had a very healthy appetite. In my first year at primary school I was chosen to play for the school football team for a match against another local school, and our biggest rivals. The games teacher started to give us a rousing team talk about tactics and so on, then stopped and asked if there were any questions so far. I was the only boy who put up his hand.

"Please, Sir, will we be having sausages and mash after the match, like the big boys do?" I asked.

"I'm sure that can be arranged," he replied, smiling.

Finally the team was over, and once again the teacher asked if there were any last-minute questions. And again I was the only boy who put up his hand.

"Sir ... how many sausages will we be having?"

Oliver Morgan

The worlde waxeth worse every day, and all is turned upside down, contrary to th'olde guyse, for all that was to me a pleasure when I was a childe, from iij yere olde to x (for now I go upon the xij yere), while I was under my father and mothers keeping, be tornyde now to tormentes and payne. For than I was wont to lye styll abedde tyll it was forth dais [late in the day], delitynge myselfe in slepe and ease. The sone sent in his beamys at the wyndowes that gave me light instead of a candle. O, what a sporte it was every mornynge when the son was upe to take my lusty pleasur betwixte the sheets, to beholde the rofe, the beamys, and the rafters of my chamber, and loke on the clothes that the chamber was hanged with! There durste no mann but he were made awake me oute of my slepe upon his owne hede while me list to slepe .... But nowe the worlde rennyth upon another whele, for nowe at five of the clocke by the moneylight I most go to my booke and lete slepe and slouthe alon, and yff oure maister hape to awake us, he bryngeth a rode stede of a candle.

Vulgaria, c1500

If you must hold yourself up to your children as an object lesson, hold

Remember Me?

"Do you remember me?" asked the young man.
The old man at the bus stop,
Shabby, standing in the sun, alone,
Looked round.
He stared for a moment, screwing up his eyes,
Then shook his head.
"No, I don't remember you."
"You used to teach me," said the young man.
"I've taught so many," said the old man, sighing,
"I forget."
"I was the boy you said was useless,
Good for nothing, a waste of space.
Who always left your classroom crying,
And dreaded every lesson that you taught."
The old man shook his head and turned away.
"No, I don't remember you," he murmured.
"Well, I remember you," the young man said.

Gervase Phinn

My lasting memory is the headmaster's parting shot: "Well, goodbye, Graves, and remember that your best friend is the waste-paper basket." This has proved good advice, though not perhaps in the sense he intended: few writers seem to send their work through as many drafts as I do.

Robert Graves

---

yourself up as a warning and not as an example. George Bernard Shaw

5. SPECIAL TIMES

When I was young, most summers the family had a week in Blackpool. Our first port of call in the town would be R H O Hills, the ice-cream parlour on the front, and Dad would treat us to a 'knickerbocker glory': that tall cone-shaped glass full of raspberry jelly, strawberries, chunks of tinned peach and different flavoured ice-creams, scattered liberally with crushed nuts and topped with a shiny glazed cherry. We would be given a long shiny metal spoon but, try as we might, we never did get that last bit of peach at the bottom of the glass.

Every morning the children would walk with Dad from the boarding house along the prom to get his paper.

"Smell the ozone," Dad would say, breathing in deeply.

If the tide was out he would sit in a deckchair on the beach to read his paper, keeping a wary eye on the three boys as we ran into the sea.

I remember vividly the swimming trunks I wore: dark green knitted affairs with a canvas belt and metal clasp which took some skill to keep on once sodden with water.

There is a picture of me with my brothers, arms around each other, shivering near the sea's edge. We had just emerged from the water and stand there in these heavy, sagging, uncomfortable outfits.

After our swim we would build the most amazing sand-castles. We were equipped for the task with brightly coloured metal spades with long wooden handles. Mine was blue, Alex's red and Michael's green. We also had substantial metal buckets and a set each of little paper flags of all the nations to stick on our creations.

You can do anything with children if you only play with them. To youth

I have but three words of counsel: Work, work, work. Bismarck

One morning we were keen to get started on our sand-castles but as we the followed Dad along the promenade we saw, much to our disappointment, that the tide was in. This put brother Michael in a tetchy mood, and he started complaining and dragging his spade behind him along the ground, making the most awful scraping noise. He was told several times by Dad to stop but he continued.

"If you do it again," said Dad almost casually, "I shall throw the spade in the sea."

Michael desisted for a while but then started again to scrape the spade along the ground. True to his word, Dad took the spade from him and hurled it into the water.

"You just threw my spade in the sea," gasped Michael.

"And if I hear any more from you," said Dad, "the bucket goes in as well."

I learnt from my father that, when an adult warns a child he will do something, then he should carry it out. It was a good lesson to learn for a prospective teacher.

Gervase Phinn

The best way to keep children home is to make the home atmosphere

A pub is an excellent place for a holiday when you are young and impressionable.

Frank Muir

The memory of seaside Sundays is strong and brilliant too. Here again, even on holiday, the hand of Methodism still took its stern grip on us. Even to set foot on the beach on the Sabbath Day was forbidden. Buckets and spades and balls and bathing drawers were put away as if they were devices of the devil. Others might trip down the steps of horse-drawn bathing cabins to disport themselves in the Sunday sea, but not us. Donkey rides, games, running, ice-creams, pop: all were taboo.

H E Bates

I never enjoyed the seaside, and I suspect the following may be the reason...

Arriving at the beach, Mother would produce my swimsuit and tell me to put it on. I hated the ghastly thing. It was bright orange and someone had knitted it for me. It was like a pair of shorts with straps and bib at the front, fastened with rubber buttons. When I wore it I looked just like a woolly Jaffa Cake.

If I kept out of the sea it was just about tolerable, but when wet I feel it is better left to the imagination than described.

Each summer it continued to fit — it sort of grew with me. After several years I discovered the power of prayer, and prayed as hard as I could that the dreaded thing would get moths.

Lo and behold, the following summer when my mother produced my swimsuit from its winter resting place, my prayers had been answered. The moths had had a great feast and rendered it unwearable.

That orange swimsuit is now a distant memory, but I cannot help feeling that it has a lot to answer for.

Gilliam Peak

pleasant -- and let the air out of the tyres. Dorothy Parker

I was proud to know that people came to my town for a holiday. It always seemed a pity that they couldn't stop the whole year round because, in those golden growing-up years, there was a sort of magic about Morecambe. It had a lot to offer and I took it.

Eric Morecambe

If variety was the spice of life, we certainly had it. In those days we bathed from vans. They were lined up on the beach and we went up about four steps to get inside. How cold and damp they were! We undressed and donned bathing suits, which were provided with the van. They were usually made of heavy blue serge, trimmed with white braid, being very high at the neck, with trousers well below the knees. We put on the bathing caps and we were ready. A tap on the door and we were moving. We looked through the small high window, and attached to the front was a horse, which dragged the van to the edge of the water. We opened our door and descended into the sea; as quickly as possible in case an ankle was seen.

Mrs M Heath

When, in 1937, we were able to afford our first seaside holiday in Bridlington, a box Brownie was obtained by the assiduous collection of coupons from other people's copies of *John Bull*. I demanded donkey rides and trips on miniature trains which we could not afford, and in the evenings I refused to go to sleep. My nocturnal enthusiasm was submerging a model deep-sea diver in the wash jug, blowing and sucking on the end of the rubber tube that came out of his head with an obsession that must have given him the plastic bends.

Roy Hattersley

The first memory I have which connected me to the outside world and the concerns of adults was the sinking of HMS *Hood*. The announcement went something like this: "It is with

There are two things that a child will share willingly —

communicable diseases and its mother's age. Dr Benjamin Spock

If he calls it a childish game, that means his wife

the deepest regret that the Admiralty announces the sinking of HMS *Hood*. No further details will be issued until the next of kin have been informed."

There were, as it turned out, only three survivors. I can remember the gloomy silence which descended on the adults in the room. Someone said: "God isn't on our side".

Mavis Holt

The rabbit was christened Adolf. We were enchanted by him. We couldn't really love him, because he was wild and loveless to the end. But he was an unmixed delight. We decided he was too small to live in a hutch — he must live at large in the house. My mother protested, but in vain. He was so tiny. We had him upstairs, and he dropped his tiny pills on the bed and we were enchanted.

D H Lawrence

I wish I had had your chances of improving myself but brothers howsoever charming they may be are expensive creatures and take all the money, and the sisters have to grow up ignorant and make their own dresses, neither of which processes is pleasant nor am I enamoured of either.

Blanch Dundas, c1850

He was quite an ordinary boy, was Henry Moore, games-loving and fun-loving. You wouldn't have singled him out as a future famous artist at all. He was quite a decent lad on the right wing at football.

Frank Ambler

We would leave in the morning to go out and play and come back when we were hungry. Grandma must have worried herself sick, or did she just not have to worry in those days?

Richard Riley

can beat him at it. American proverb

Eche time and season hath its delite and joyes,
Loke in the streets beolde the little boyes
Howe in fruite season for joy they sing and hop;
In Lent is eche one full busy with his top,
And nowe in winter for all the grievous colde,
All rent and ragged a man may them beholde,
They have great pleasour, supposing well to dine,
When men be busied in killing of fat swine.
They get the bladder and blowe it great and thin,
With many beans or peasen put within;
It ratleth, soundeth and shineth clere and fayre
When it is thrown and caste up in the ayre.
Eche one contendeth and hath a great delite
With foote and with hande the bladder for to smite.
If it fall to grounde they lifte it up agayne,
This wise to labour they count it for no payne,
Renning and leaping they drive away the colde.

Alexander Barclay, c1520

Between five and thirteen, roughly, you play with your own sex. Games change as the year unfolds, following the products of the season (eg 'conkers'), or simply by the boys' own intuitively followed rhythm.

At one time everyone is playing 'taws', with his marbles ranked in prestige according to age and killing power; quite suddenly marbles go and everybody wants a threepenny peashooter ... Hops and shuttlecocks have almost entirely gone, and whips-and-tops are not so popular now; but 'piseball', 'tig', hopscotch across the flags and a great number of games involving running round the lamp-posts or in and out of the closet-areas, such as 'Cowboys and Indians', are still popular.

Girls still like skipping-ropes, and almost peculiar to them is the game of dressing-up — trailing round the streets in grown-ups' cast-off clothes and old lace, as 'a wedding' ...

Children have never been very good at listening to their elders, but

they have never failed to imitate them. James Baldwin

There are outings with jam-jars to a dirty stream a mile or so away, for sticklebacks and red-throats ...

Those who can cadge a few coppers from their mothers go to the public baths; or occasionally catch a tram to some remote part of the city where the children's playground is said to be good, and spend the whole day there with a few sandwiches and a bottle of pop between the lot of them.

Professor Richard Hoggart

The Ecchoing Green

The Sun does arise,
And make happy the skies;
The merry bells ring,
To welcome the Spring;
The sky-lark and thrush,
The birds of the bush,
Sing louder around
To the bells' cheerful sound,
While our sports shall be seen
On the Ecchoing Green.

Old John, with white hair,
Does laugh away care,
Sitting under the oak,
Among the old folk,
Hey laugh at our play,
And soon they all say;
'Such, such were the joys,
When we all, girls & boys,
In our youth time were seen,
On the Ecchoing Green.

William Blake

There's nothing sadder in this world than to awake on

One of the games we played was 'duffs'. One of the boys would duff you to do something — jump across a stream for instance. The main difference between this and a 'dare' was that he had to do it first. This struck me as a much fairer way of doing things.

Richard Riley

St Cuthbert loved games and pranks, and as was natural at his age, loved to play with other children ... He used to boast that he had beaten all those of his own age and many who were older at wrestling, jumping, running, and every other exercise.

Venerable Bede

When mere children, as soon as they could read and write, Charlotte, and her brother and sisters, used to invent and act little plays of their own, in which the Duke of Wellington, my Daughter Charlotte's Hero, was sure to come off the conquering hero — when a dispute would not infrequently arise amongst them regarding the comparative merits of him, Buonaparte, Hannibal, and Caesar —When the argument got warm, and rose to its height, as their mother was then dead, I had sometimes to come in as arbitrator, and settle the dispute, according to the best of my judgement.

Patrick Brontë

When the other three brothers, preluding the pursuits of manhood in their childish play, were tracing or building, in sand or dust, now towns, now places, he himself, in like prophetic play, was ever busy with all his might in designing churches or building monasteries.

'Autobiography of Gerald of Wales', c1160

Girls have their needlework, their Dolls, and are content ... The boy is the father to the man, and as men have to rough it

---

Christmas morning and not be a child. Erma Bombeck

My first rule of consumerism is never to buy anything

in the outer world, and fight their way to the post of honour that they may select for their goal, so the sports of boys must of necessity be rough, to prepare them for their future turbulent career.

Trevethen Spicer, 1855

My brothers' practice was, when they met together, to exercise themselves with fencing, wrestling, shooting and suchlike exercises, for I observed they did seldom hawk or hunt, and very seldom or never dance, or play on music, saying it was too effeminate for masculine spirits ... As for the pastimes of my sisters when they were in the country, it was to read, work, walk, and discourse with each other.

Margaret Cavendish, c1640

I remember 'Spanish Wine Day', when the children all had their bottles. The wine was made of 'Spanish' — a stick of black liquorice (which the shops kept especially for the purpose) and dissolved in water and continually shaken.

John Townsend

Ma and Pa Pearson told me that one Sunday, during a thunderstorm, lightning had struck the window area and a knife on the table, causing it to fly across the room and stick into the solid wall on the other side.

As a precaution we always placed cutlery under the table-cloth during thunderstorms and drew the curtains. During bad storms, Mum and I went and hid under the stairs.

John Iveson

Taken to the circus as a small boy, Alan Ayckbourn was terrified by the grotesque make-up of a clown, and bit him. He has been wary of audience participation ever since.

Paul Allen

---

you can't make your children carry. Bill Bryson

The railway construction depot up the hill provided excellent play facilities; there were tall heaps of sand to run up and down and flatten, bags of cement to jump on and kick into grey clouds, heavy nuts and bolts to hurl at the watchman's hut, and best of all, an old, slow-moving and bad-tempered watchman to provoke.

One evening Mother asked us what plans we had for the morning. We said, "We're going to the builders' depot to play with the Bugger-Off Man."

Frank Muir

My father became interested in beekeeping in the early 1940s, when I was still a boy, and he developed his hobby until he had an apiary of twenty hives. Bees, their equipment and their management through the seasons virtually took over our household.

One day I was helping to remove queen cells, but had not realised I had tucked my beekeeping veil into an aertex shirt — a recipe for disaster! I beat a hasty retreat, but not before getting thirty stings through the holes in my shirt. Fortunately I was not allergic, and I sometimes wonder — since bee stings have been used as treatments for rheumatic joints — if I built up a resistance to rheumatism by being stung as a boy.

John Chippendale

In my childhood, Christmas did not begin several months beforehand. Only a week or at most a fortnight before the day did the two village shop-windows sport paper and tinsel decorations, cotton-wool snow sprinkled with 'frost', and those stockings of coarse canvas through which their contents look so much more inviting than they really are.

Ruth Hedger

How can there be too many children? That is like saying

there are too many flowers. Mother Teresa

Dad was employed at Christmas in one of the big chain stores as 'The one and only Santa Claus'. Dad had to sit all day at the end of a hot, dimly lit tunnel. This made him so thirsty that I had to take him a pint of beer every dinnertime on my way back to school. He would hide the bottle under his greasy red robe, and take a swig when trade was slack. I never had any illusions about Father Christmas after that.

Nicholas Charles

Christmas was...

It was a white goose, limp
on the back seat of a Morris Eight
and Father coping with it in the coal-house.
It was Mother icing the cake
while frying sausages.
It was attic secrets and used-before paper.
It was snapping evergreens in a frosty wood.
The sap-scented tree in a bucket
darkening the room, but thrilling.
It was trying to find the dead fairy-light
that spoiled the illuminations
of a ten-bulb string.
It was waking to feel for the soft sock
in the morning, and the smell
of a thumbnail sharp with tangerine.
It was church, and wondering
about the ordinary, grey things:
streets, pavements, winter sky,
and why they were not touched with colour
just for this one day.

Hilary Shields

Always end the name of your child with a vowel, so that

when you yell it, the name will carry. Bill Cosby

Shortly before Christmas each year an important event took place — the annual goose killings. Neighbours often came to help with both the plucking and the dressing, and help was given in return.

We, being the younger members of the family, acted as carriers to keep the dressers supplied with plucked geese.

Dressing a goose had to be done thoroughly. When the windpipes were removed, we children used them as 'squeakers', by blowing through them.

Feather stripping was an occupation reserved for the wild days of winter when no outside work was possible. Holding the tip of the feathers in the left hand, they were stripped off both sides of the centre rib, which was then thrown onto the hearth to be burnt on the fire.

In imagination I can still smell the pungent fumes from the burning quills.

John Chippendale

I have fond recollections of childhood Christmases. Ever at the mercy of the seasons, the clothing we wore in December was different to that of any of the preceding months. Python-like mufflers reminiscent of stage-coach days. Hand-knitted woollen gloves that could have been made for sloths. Balaclavas. Rasping vests. Worsted overcoats. Fair Isle sweaters. Heavy grey cotton shirts and wool socks thicker than pipe lagging would suddenly appear from their darkling sabbatical at the back of the wardrobe to engulf us young Truemans in a haze of mothballs and lavender.

I can recall the wonderful mixture of excitement, anticipation and joy that swept through my body on awaking to find a large Christmas stocking hanging from the post at the end of my bed. The sock would bulge as if holding a leg suffering from the worst case of varicose veins and arthritic lumps imaginable.

I thank the goodness and the grace, Which in my birth have smiled,

"He's been!" I would cry at the top of my voice, much to the chagrin of my slumbering parents. In my stocking there would be toys in boxes on which was emblazoned 'CWS' — the mark that they had came from the Co-operative Welfare Society.

Also in my stocking there might be a colouring book and some coloured pencils, perhaps a rubber ball, a classic children's book such as *Treasure Island* and always an orange, apple or some nuts. Compared to what youngsters receive today, the contents of my Christmas stocking might appear frugal, though I never thought it to be. On the contrary, I was always overjoyed by what I received and a simple rubber tennis ball, colouring book and pencils would afford me countless hours of entertainment. They were simple presents that gave simple pleasures.

Fred Trueman

Then, in bed, fighting to sleep and to forget the miracle of the Christmas morning to come. Saying, if I get a farm with cows and sheep and a five-bar gate and chickens and a coop and a metal stream and a few trees about the place and a green field made of billiard cloth and a dog or two and a cat — never mind the cat — and perhaps a fox on a hill ... if I get this, with a pair of ball-bearing roller stakes so that I can gleam and flash and go backwards through the heavy Friday traffic and be as glamorous as Boy Davids from the Park.... If I get those things and a book or two — I will go to Wednesday night chapel for a whole year. And I got them and I did!

One year I topped everybody. My brother gave me a beautiful bicycle — hub-braked and dynamoed, a thing of beauty and a joy for a couple or three years. I have never ceased to be proud of that winged machine. I allowed everybody to ride it. I went to Swansea on it and Newport. I cycled on it to Aberdare and Mountain Ash.

Richard Burton

And made me in these Christian days, A happy English child. Ann Taylor

For such a child I blesse God, in whose bosom he is! May I

Everyone must remember that dreadful winter of 1947, but being young my younger brothers and I enjoyed it — no school for me for starters, and my father at home more than at work was able to take three of us and the dog through snow-drifts unheard of in today's world.

I think my mother must have been made to let him be in charge of two tiny toddlers and myself aged eight. She used to say the dog was less trouble than the three of us together.

Dinah C M Brown

I loved the heavy winter snows which are now, it seems, a childhood experience seldom to be repeated.

The winters of the early war years were fierce. I recall the hard, steely skies breeding blizzards from the east and three continuous days of snow filling the croft which formed a terrace outside our home.

I hated the warm west winds which blew down the valley from Lancashire, inducing a thaw and removing the country-side's romantic white blanket. I can still hardly bear to spoil the beauty of freshly fallen snow.

Sir Bernard Ingham

When ice-sliding, the gentle slope of the playground helped to speed up one's progress but the two steps down into the garden required a good deal of practice to ensure keeping upright.

The beginner was wise to join a 'train', which consisted of some dozen boys who held on to each other.

Now and again there was an accident, resulting in a grand collapse and then it was a case of picking yourself up as quick-ly as possible so as to clear the track.

Occasionally the headmaster granted an extra allowance of playtime, greatly to the delight of the sliders.

J A Barringer

---

and mine become as this little child. John Evelyn

Bonfire Night

I remember my first Bonfire Night.
It was cold and clear, and the air smelled of smoke.
My father sat me high on his shoulders to see
The dancing flames
And the red sparks spitting in the air.
My face burned with the heat.
And then I saw him —
The figure sitting on the wigwam of wood.
I screamed and screamed and screamed.
"There's a man on top," I cried, "a man in the fire!
Oh help him, Daddy, please!"
And everyone laughed.
"It's just the guy," my father said.
"He's made of rags and paper.
He's not real."
But I was sad and scared to see
Those clinging fingers of fire
Scorch the stuffed body, crackling the arms,
Those searing tongues of flame lick round
The bloated legs,
And swallow up the wide-eyed, smiling face.

Gervase Phinn

There was always a good circus held behind the church in a field. How I did love them and seeing the procession of the animals come up the town before the afternoon performance. Camels, elephants and zebras, and one circus had a huge caravan with bars across a slit for windows with some wild Indians or Patagonians in — we could see their big frizzy heads dancing about in the van. I must say I have a sneaking fondness for a circus even now.

Eva Wise

A very rich person should leave his kids enough to do anything

The local magician, Mr Bull, who used to entertain at all the York children's parties, was less entranced by Judi Dench. "I used to know his act, so I used to say, 'Watch, watch, here comes the rabbit'. So he said to the hostess, 'I'm absolutely not doing my act if she's there, because she ruins it'. Poor man, can you imagine? I can't imagine anything worse."

John Miller

"How I wish I were a boy!" Mother caught me saying this aloud one day, and promptly told me that this was a wicked thought. She did not go on to give a reason, but merely insisted that it was splendid to be a girl, and with such exuberant enthusiasm that I was quite convinced. My father's slogan was that boys should go everywhere and know everything, and that a girl should stay at home and know nothing ... The boys used to go to the theatre and music-halls. The latter sounded rather dull, but mother explained that they were not dull, only not very nice. However, it made no difference to me what they were like, since I was never allowed to go even to a theatre.

Molly Hughes, c1880

The young people made much of St Valentine's Day. We girls seldom knew who sent us the pretty token, for dales lads were a bit shy in their lovemaking. I treasured one valentine for many years solely because I admired the picture — two birds looking at a nest in a flowery bower of trees. Some verses underneath this began:

I have built in my fancy a little nest,
As the birds build theirs in the trees;
It is furnished with love for one I love best,
And thought of happiness borne on the breeze.

I never knew who sent this and I never tried to find out. Every girl treated her valentines with the same indifference but, all the same, she would have been sadly disappointed had they

but not enough to do nothing. Warren Buffett

failed to arrive. Actually, the valentine had little to do with lovemaking. The lads sent them to the lassies they knew as a gesture of friendship. The great thing was for a girl to be able to boast of how many she got.

Mabel Horner Thompson

It's difficult to convey the full horror of the all-girls' party to those who have not experienced it themselves. About half the girls who attended had already decided they were going to be the best dressed, the one who won prizes and the one who screamed loudest.

"Here comes trouble!" thought my mother as they flounced through the door.

Yet this party was by far the least violent of all I had. The girls had not yet got into the full swing of devilry.

Fiona Pitt-Kethley

I remember seeing an escapologist perform on a bombsite covered in cinders. His whole body was wrapped in chains, padlocked together, and he stepped inside a big kitbag that was locked with another chain. He started rolling around on the ground, wriggling and kicking up cinders. This seemed to go on for ages until we heard him groan. Finally this plaintive voice from inside the sack said: "Can you get me out? I've swallowed the friggin' key."

Ricky Tomlinson

September 1939 was hot, and lots of mothers had taken small children to the local park. Suddenly the air-raid warning siren sounded for the very first time. The park emptied in seconds. It may only have been a practice, but everyone scattered. After the all-clear sounded, my mother had to run back to collect the knitting she had left on a park bench. It was still there.

Mavis Holt

I love children, especially when they cry, because

then somebody tales them away. Nancy Mitford

There was mirth even in evacuation. I recall a group of my friends saying a tearful goodbye to mums as they boarded buses in Leeds to take them to the safety of far-away Tadcaster. It must have been all of fourteen miles away from home. But it seemed like the other side of the world to mothers and offspring, who embraced as though they would never again have the opportunity to clasp each other. Before I could join in the adventure, my mates returned. The powers that be decided Leeds was a much safer place than Tadcaster and families were happily reunited.

John Morgan

In spring we made ourselves useful by gathering leaves of the sweet dock in the mowing meadows until the end of April. They were worth six old pence per full carrier bag on the open market.

Sweet dock was the basic ingredient for dock pudding — a boiling of docks, nettle tips, spring onions and oatmeal, eventually served fried with bacon.

During the war, dock pudding not only cleansed our blood — its reputed purpose in earlier days of a relatively deprived winter diet — but also raised our morale. The traitor, Lord Haw Haw, broadcast from Germany that we were starving in the North and reduced to eating grass. Grass, my foot. We were feasting on ambrosia.

Sir Bernard Ingham

There was a huge potato pile in the field as a result of the 'Dig for Victory Campaign'. The Ministry of Agriculture never arrived to collect them and the potatoes were eventually used for pig swill. We used to put small potatoes on springy willow sticks and launch them huge distances down the field, placing spikes to mark the length of the throw. Michael Brown, my friend and school mate, was the champion spud thrower.

The trouble with children is that they're

So much for the Dig for Victory effort! In our imaginative way we thought that the spud throwing, catapult stones, and Stan in the Home Guard with his helmet and farm shotgun were more than a match for the Germans.

John Iveson

The back gardens of our terrace and of the one opposite were separated by a narrow lane — a 'ginnel' we called it — which met a slightly wider lane in a T-junction a few yards from our back gate. This was our playground, an area for football and marbles under the gaslight in winter, and for cricket, always cricket, in the summer. The thought that we might have played anything else never occurred to us. Tennis and golf were upper-middle-class games that needed fancy equipment, special clothes and preferably fancy accents.

Geoffrey Boycott

Taws [marbles] were as popular with Yorkshire lads as beddy, tig and kick-out can. Colourful glass 'alleys' were prized possessions, and so were 'stonkers', made, as the name suggests, from stone.

John Morgan

Looking back I am intrigued by the terminology we then used without thinking it in any way strange.

For instance, marbles were 'taws' to us. When we played to keep our gains we were playing 'for'. When we 'knuckled' from knee or hip height that was called 'plonking', and if successful was considered the height of prowess. If an opponent jerked his hand forward when knuckling he was promptly accused of 'fullocking', which wasn't playing the game. Sometimes the 'knuckle taw' would shoot a marble out of the ring and stop dead in its place, spinning round at the same time. It was then said to have 'spun fat'.

not returnable. Quentin Crisp

The child that is not clean and neat, With lots of toys and things to eat,

If a lad had 'shigged' his partner of all his marbles he would, perhaps out of pity, or as a salve to conscience, sometimes offer to 'dit' him in, that is, he would give him a chance to start again by putting a few marbles in the ring for him.

J Laycock

A game of marbles started with one player 'plugging' his taw on the pitch. His rival would fire from the ledge, and experts gripped the taw between thumb and finger to propel the aerial onslaught from raised knee-cap. If he hit the target, he then aimed for the 'knack', and if his taw dropped in a hole he collected his rival's 'alley'. But there were tricks to render the simple exercise difficult. You have to be as quick with the tongue as the taw. If you shouted "No rounds, tibs, bonks, bobs or over", the opposing player could not hit your taw and had to play a safety shot. You were sometimes accused of 'sticking your neb', which meant you advanced the knuckle beyond the accepted point of delivery.

John Morgan

'Gaffers.' There were not many rules connected with this game. The 'gaffer' was armed with a very strong whip. It was wise to get out of the way. If caught, one had to stand with hands raised above the head to receive several strokes. It was wise to button your coat and hope for the best.

J A Barringer

Thirty years ago [1909] when the children at Askrigg prepared to start a game that required one particular individual to take some important part, they used this counting-out rhyme:
"Oakum, bocum, stony cokum,
Ellerkin, bellerkin, bony bush,
Out goes he."

R M Chapman

He is a naughty child, I'm sure – Or else his dear pap is poor. R L Stevenson

Lads' hobbies in the early 1900s often revolved around a hutch or a pen. Pictured are Herbert and Arthur Jarman of Keighley with their prize-winning guinea pigs. When the Jarman brothers commemorated this success, they went, not to a fashionable portrait studio, but to Amos Dewhirst, a local newsagent and stationer, and amateur photographer, who contrived this appealing effect with one cup, two boys, three guinea pigs and a box on a table. Young Arthur Jarman was to die of smallpox at Basra during the First World War.

Ian Dewhirst

There is no magic on earth strong enough to wipe out

When I was a lad we couldn't wait for the cricket season to start. Every street was a Test Match arena. Every available wall had stumps and bails chalked on it.

Balls did not have leather cases. They were 'corkies' with a ridged seam and they quickly lost their coat of red paint. They were lethal missiles in the hands of mates who hurled them with scant regard for the safety of lads whose only protection was a roughly hewn bat.

Do you remember those home-made bats? I had one cut and shaped from paling broken from a dilapidated fence. When it connected with the corky ball, a thousand electric shocks shot up the arm. Your hands — and brain, if any — went numb. And they stayed that way until life returned with a bout of tingling pins and needles.

Few lads lasted more than one over, and my monstrosity of a bat finished its days sailing down the local beck.

John Morgan

Give me the works which delighted my youth. Give me the *History of St George* and the *Seven Champions of Christendom*, which at every leisure moment I used to hide myself in a corner to read. Give me the *Arabian Nights' Entertainments*, which I used to watch till the sun shining on the bookcase approached it, and glowing full upon it gave me courage to take it from the shelf.

Samuel Taylor Coleridge

Being country people, our lives were very much governed by the seasons. Boyhood life for me was cyclical. Summer and autumn fused into one another almost always imperceptibly. I could never remember the actual day summer turned into autumn, the point of fusion was invariably lost some time in mid-September.

Fred Trueman

the legacies of one's parents. Salman Rushdie

In imitation of the Savages described in *Robinson Crusoe* or some other Savages, I often, in a morning, set off stark naked across the Fell where I was joined by some associates, who in like manner, ran about like mad things.

Thomas Bewick

In late summer we roamed the hillsides gathering bilberries. This was a tedious business because of its tiny fruit but it was richly rewarded when my mother served it in a flaky suet pudding with white sauce. My mouth waters at the mere memory of it.

Sir Bernard Ingham

We got our first car in 1954 when I was six — the car was two years older. A black Morris 8, it had no heaters, and we needed blankets and hot-water bottles in winter.

In contrast, it had every sort of ventilation imaginable. Even the windscreen opened. It also had a sliding roof, but it was very stiff.

One day it was wide open when a thunderstorm broke and, no matter how we tugged, it wouldn't shut. Mum solved the problem by sticking her umbrella out through the hole. It must have looked comical, but we didn't get wet.

Hazel Martell

As far as I was concerned, going to Cleethorpes or Skegness was like travelling to the other side of the world.

Fred Trueman

Judi Dench's reputation for jokes, now usually indulged by her famous colleagues, was less fondly regarded by the young men of York. One little boy named James Conyers would not even stay for one party, saying loudly for all to hear: "If Judi Dench is here, I'm going, and taking my brother with me".

John Miller

If you have never been hated by your child

I can't remember much about birthdays — we never had a birthday party or a present. Everybody was poor.

Mary Jane Dryden

As a boy I was a keen cyclist and would often journey to the Yorkshire Dales. When it was time to turn back to the mills of the West Riding in the afternoon, I used to feel a real sadness.

Patrick Stewart

For us life held far more excitement than watching the traffic lights change in Morecambe or the Co-op bacon slicer in Heckmondwike.

Austin Mitchell MP

Inspired by these films, I convinced a mate of mine, Davey Steele, that we should put on a show for the neighbourhood kids and charge them a penny at the door. I walked the streets banging on a metal drum to publicise the show, while Davey hung a sack for the curtain in the loft over his garage. The audience were literally packed to the rafters as I donned one of Mam's frocks and did my own version of Old Mother Riley.

This was my first experience of acting — unless you count trying to con my little brothers into doing chores for me. From memory it wasn't a bravura performance, but none of the kids asked for their money back. Most of them were included in the show, which proved a clever ploy. I've been improvising ever since.

Ricky Tomlinson

For the Queen's Coronation celebration, all the local children dressed in crepe paper costumes on floats, which had to be judged under cover because it rained. All the children were presented with coronation spoons; I still have mine.

Tony Law

you have never been a parent. Bette Davis

In keeping with my new role as the family jester, my brother
Chas gave me for my birthday a joke inkblot, a piece of metal
pressed into the shape of a large shiny blot of Stephen's blue-
black ink and suitably coloured. It was startlingly realistic.

Sniggering with excitement, I laid it on Mother's new carpet, put an empty ink bottle on its side beside the blot and
called out, "Quick, Mother, I've had an accident!"

Mother shot in from the kitchen, took in the sight of the ink
bottle on its side and the large blot on her beautiful new carpet, and gave me a whack round the back of my head with her
wedding-ring finger which sent me ricocheting off three walls.

This would probably have won her fourteen days' hard
labour in Holloway Prison in these enlightened times but it
was exactly the right treatment then. I have hated the lurking
sadism of practical joking ever since.

Frank Muir

One of my favourite tricks was to tie black cotton to a door-
knocker in the street and then trail it across the road to a hid-
ing place in one of the entries.

I tugged the cotton.

"Knock, knock."

Mrs Stringer, a fifties version of Hyacinth Bouquet, opened
the door, looked up and down the street and then closed it
again.

I waited half a second.

"Knock, knock."

The trick was to see how many times I could do it before
she caught on and snapped the cotton. No matter what door
I targeted and how well I hid, the reaction was always the
same.

"I know it's you, Ricky Tomo, you little shite. I'm gonna tell
your Mam."

Ricky Tomlinson

Sing out loud in the car even, or especially,

There was no telly, though that didn't mean we explored the world instead; we either shot at it or threw stones at it.

Austin Mitchell MP

At chapel the preachers often "shouted to God" during the sermons, and Mum told me it was because God was sometimes "a long way off and a bit deaf".

John Iveson

The vocal enthusiasm of the congregation and the charismatic nature of the service made a deep impression on my brother Chas and me. So much so that back home, halfway through lunch, Chas suddenly leaped to his feet and declaimed very loudly, "Alleluia!" Then he sat down, leaving our two stunned parents looking at each other. Not to be outdone and now well in the mood of the meeting, a few minutes later I too leaped to my feet, eyes shining with zeal. "God be praised!" I announced ringingly. "Can I have another potato?"

Frank Muir

When my brother John had his tonsils out, one post-operative treatment was having frequent ice-cream. Due to shortages and John's needs, I didn't get any. To add insult to injury, I had to go to the shop for it. When I was due to have my tonsils out, the first disappointment was not going to Leeds to the pantomime. It was Norman Evans who dressed as a woman and had conversations 'over the garden wall'. But the biggest blow was that it was no longer the practice to indulge in ice cream; what a liberty.

Richard Riley

As a child I delighted in bran-tubs. One never knew what a quick delving into the sawdust might produce.

Rebecca Hey

if it embarrasses your children. Marilyn Penland

6. BEST AND WORST OF TIMES

Brenda (I have changed the name to save any embarrassment) was my first date. I was fifteen and I met her through my friend, Peter. He was 'walking out' with a strikingly pretty, dark-haired girl called Lynne, and she had this friend, a small, round-faced strawberry blonde, called Brenda. I agreed to meet Brenda in the Ring o' Bells Café in Rotherham and we would go to the cinema.

I spent a good hour getting ready, scrubbing my face until it shone, brushing my teeth violently, slicking down my hair with Brylcreem, splashing my brother's aftershave liberally over face and body, changing my shirt umpteen times, squeezing into tight drainpipe trousers and polishing my winkle-pickers to a high shine. When I looked in the bathroom mirror I thought I looked quite presentable.

Brenda sat in the corner on the café dressed in a bright pink knitted cardigan and wearing sensible brown sandals and white ankle socks.

"Hello," I said.

"Hello," she replied.

"Want a drink?" I asked.

"Milkshake," she said. "Strawberry. Large one."

That was pretty much the extent of the conversation until we arrived at the Tivoli Cinema to join the queue for the film.

"So, what do you like doing?" I asked her.

"Knitting."

"Oh."

"I've knitted this cardigan. Do you like it?"

"Yes."

"Don't your feet hurt in those shoes?" she asked.

"No."

"I'll knit you a scarf if you want."

"Great."

I bought Brenda a large packet of popcorn and she sat through the first part of *The Amazing Colossal Man* munching away merrily. The film was a version of *King Kong* but set in the atomic age. This colonel was exposed to a massive dose of radiation during a nuclear bomb test and mutated into a fearsome giant.

In those days girls were inclined to scream and boys whoop really loudly when anything frightening appeared on the screen. If there was a romantic part, particularly one involving kissing, there would be great jeers, howls and kissing noises from the audience, and some brave boy would shout out "Gerrem off!".

Brenda sat there motionless, her eyes glued to the screen, posting popcorn into her mouth, which she crunched noisily. When she had consumed the entire packet she suddenly thrust her face forward and planted her lips on mine. This occurred a few times before the lights came up. It was a quick, unexpected, jerky, popcorn-tasting experience.

"Are we having chips?" she asked, as I walked her home.

"If you want."

"I like scraps," said Brenda.

Scraps were the bits of fried batter which came away from the fish and were given away free.

I asked for two four-pennyworth of chips and scraps.

"Do you like scraps?" she asked.

"Yes I do."

"What fish are you having?"

"I'm not having any."

"I like cod."

"I'm not that hungry."

glad to get him asleep. Ralph Waldo Emerson

"You can have a bit of my cod if you want."

"Thanks."

"Are you having mushy peas?"

"No."

"I am. You can have some of those as well."

"Thanks."

I said goodbye to her at the gate but kept my distance. I didn't want to be pounced on again.

"Bye," I said.

"I'll get started on your scarf," she told me.

That was my first fleeting romance. It was a 'brief encounter', for I found that scraps were the only thing we had in common.

Gervase Phinn

But the memories that seem important to remember are not of these chance touchings of the skirts of history, but of quite simple things, drifting snowflakes seen through a melted peephole in a frost nursery window, the sun like a red-hot penny in the smoky Leeds sky, and the dreadful screaming of a wounded hare. That last I can never forget.

Arthur Ransome

Adolf Hitler did his best to overshadow my arrival. There I was, snug and cosy, with nothing better to do than head-butt Mam's bladder five times a night, when he decided to invade Poland. It's amazing what some people will do to compensate for having only one ball.

Ricky Tomlinson

Once I had found a way out of my confinement, nothing was going to stop me as I found a variety of ways to get myself out and about to cause parental palpitations. If I was left outside

There's no point in being grown up if you

the house in my pram, brake or no brake, I would bounce it
up and down until I eventually succeeded in getting the thing
moving. I managed to cover some fairly impressive distances
but, luckily, everyone knew who I was and where to return me.

Ian Botham

Infant Joy

"I have no name: I am but two days old."

What shall I call thee?
"I happy am.
Joy is my name."
Sweet joy befall thee!

Pretty joy!
Sweet joy, but two days old!
Sweet joy I call thee.
Thou dost smile.
I sing the while.
Sweet joy befall thee!

William Blake

When my children were very young, when as far as I can
remember, the oldest was about ten years of age and the
youngest about four — thinking that they knew more, than I
had yet discovered, in order to make them speak with less
timidity, I deemed that if they were put under a sort of cover,
I might gain my end — and happening to have a mask in the
house, I told them all to stand, and speak boldly from under
the mask — I began with the youngest — I asked what a child
like her most wanted — she answered, age and experience —
I asked the next what I had best do with her brother Branwell,
what was the best way of knowing the difference between the
intellects, of men and women — he answered by considering
the difference between them as to their bodies — I then asked

can't be childish sometimes. Dr Who

Charlotte, what was the best book in the world, she answered, the Bible — and what was the next best, she answered the Book of Nature — I then asked the next, what was the best mode of education for a woman, she answered, that which would make her rule her house well — Lastly I asked the oldest, what was the best mode of spending time, she answered, by laying it out in preparation for a happy eternity — I may not have given precisely their words, but I have nearly done so as they made a deep and lasting impression on my memory.

Patrick Brontë

My earliest childhood memory is of the first day I was able to dress myself. It was a hot June morning. Apart from underwear, I wore a white cotton dress sprigged with roses and fastened with three press-studs, with white socks and black patent strap shoes. I must have been about three. I remember how impressed my parents were, as I had dressed before they were up. I have liked warm early summer mornings ever since.

Mavis Holt

Most people who believe in the institution of childhood as we know it see it as a kind of walled garden in which children, being small and weak, are protected from the harshness of the world outside until they become strong and clever enough to cope with it. Some children experience childhood in just that way. I do not want to destroy their garden or kick them out of it. If they like it, by all means let them stay in it. But I believe that most young people, and at earlier and earlier ages, begin to experience childhood not as a garden but as a prison ... I am not saying that childhood is bad for all children all the time. But Childhood, as in Happy, Safe, Protected, Innocent Childhood, does not exist for many children. For many other children, however good it may be, childhood goes on far too long.

John Holt

If we are to reach real peace in this world, we shall

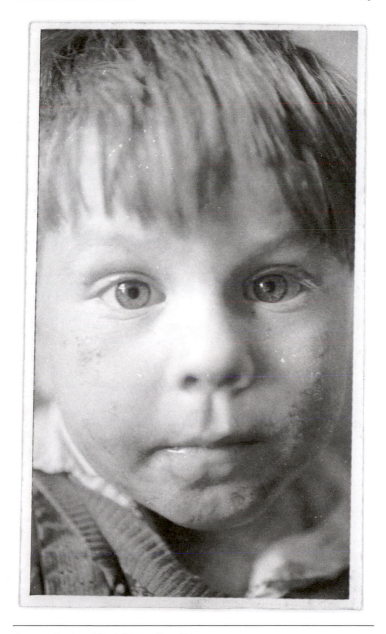

have to begin with children. Gandhi

Childhood Dream

Ah'll hev a pirate ship an' crew,
Ah'll swank abaht on t' deck,
Wi' trusty sword an' bobby's hat.
When Ah grow up — by heck!

Ah'll slide me feet; sa'n't brush me hair,
Ah'll save fowk off a wreck,
An' do baht flippin' han'kerchief,
When Ah grow up — by heck!

Ah'll stamp me feet i' puddles too,
An' swim i' onny beck,
Ah'll stop aht late — 'til after dark,
When Ah grow up — by heck!

Ah'll live o' buns, ne'er goa ter bed,
An' nivver wesh me neck.
Hey! That's me muther callin' me.
Ah'll ne'er grow up — Aw heck!

Will Clemence

Wakes were a custom — and an accepted part of living and
dying. The immediate hours on the morning of the funeral
saw the laughter give way to tears and sobs. Men stood
bare-headed as the cortège prepared to move from the house
and head for church. Ladies folded black shawls round their
head and shoulders, and the hymns — almost inaudible at
first — grew into a wailing crescendo which sent shivers up
the spine. The eerie sound lives with me today when I dwell
on those scenes of death and distress.

John Morgan

To lose one parent may be regarded as a misfortune;

to lose both looks like carelessness. Oscar Wilde

On and off, I've been very near a twelvemonth in the streets. Before that, I had to take care of a baby for my aunt. No, it wasn't heavy — it was only two months old; but I minded it for ever such a time — till it could walk. It was a very nice little baby, not a very pretty one; but, if I touched it under the chin, it would laugh.

Before I had the baby, I used to help mother, who was in the fur trade; and, if there was any slits in the fur, I'd sew them up. My mother learned me to needle-work and to knit when I was about five. I used to go to school, too; but I wasn't there long.

Sometimes I make a great deal of money. One day I took 1s 6d, and the creases cost 6d; but it isn't often I get such luck as that. I oftener makes 3d or 4d than 1s; and then I'm at work, crying, "Creases, four bunches a penny, creases!" from six in the morning to about ten.

All my money I earns I puts in a club and draws it out to buy clothes with. It's better than spending it in sweet-stuff, for them as has a living to earn. Besides it's like a child to care for sugar-sticks, and not like one who's got a living and vitals to earn.

I ain't a child and I shan't be a woman till I'm twenty, but I'm past eight, I am.

'The little watercress girl', 1864

I am ful young
I was born yesterday
Deth is ful hasty
On me to been wreke
And of his strok
List make no delay
I cam but now
And now I go my way.

fifteenth-century 'Dance of Death'

Parents who are afraid to put their foot down will have

We children lived very close to life and knew of death. We heard what the older people said and feared. Nothing was hidden from us. We could not escape hearing.

Mabel Horner Thompson

We were severely treated. We were punished for talking — we had to sit and hold our tongues between our fingers if we talked when we shouldn't. If we talked after we'd been put to bed, they came and pulled the sheets over our heads, and I was always afraid of the dark.

By the time I was four, I was no longer considered to be a child. I had to help look after the young ones, make the cots, just generally prove useful.

The food was a penance. Monday, Wednesday and Saturday, we had watery soup, a slice of bread, and then a suet pudding with syrup. The smell of it was repelling. I often didn't eat it. We used to keep it and put it at the rat-holes, so the rats waxed fat on it.

Hetty Day in Reedham Asylum for Fatherless Children, 1929

If there is one thing I miss about my childhood life, it's the simplicity.

Fred Trueman

It surprised me to find that children were beaten as a matter of course, not just with hands but straps, even the buckle end of belts. One friend developed a severe stammer which he still has. Another was beaten by his father for not doing as well at school as his brother. I don't remember dad hitting me, but I do remember mum had a very stinging hand across the back of the legs. I felt it more often than my brother as he was possibly quieter and better behaved. I didn't know when to stop and pushed mum too far.

Richard Riley

children who step on their toes. Chinese proverb

My mother loved children — she would have given

My love for my mother had never been obsessive; it was the normal warm trust, respect and love of son for mother and vice versa. Mother had always been there, a permanent source of comfort and safety in a world often difficult to understand.

Then, lying in bed one night, it occurred to me that Mother would not always be there. One day she would die and I would never see her again. This was much too enormous a concept for my tiny split-pea brain to cope with calmly and I simply gave way to inconsolable misery, sobbing into the pillow far into the night.

Night after night for about two weeks, as I lay in bed, the dread black thought crept back that one day Mother would not be there; it was like a medieval nightmare crouching over me. I just did not know what to do but to howl as quietly as possible and hope that sleep would soon bring oblivion.

Mother chose a good moment and gave me a gentle talking-to, explaining that I was quite right about her having to leave us one day, but that was how it all worked and I must learn to accept death as a fact that none of us could do much about.

Suddenly, a few days later, as if the sun had emerged from behind a cloud, everything became all right again and life returned to being warm and secure, dread evaporated and my strange emotional and irrational experience was over; it never returned.

Frank Muir

Children of the gutter roam about free, and are often hungry, but what would one not give for such appetites? Sometimes I wonder whether they don't lead the happier lives?

Phil May, 1896

We weren't physically abused, but not once can I remember any affection being shown. You had to accept a way of life so foreign, so disciplined... I think I was always hungry.

Ed Cousins, Barnardo's boy, 1916

anything if I had been one. Groucho Marx

Leaving Home

When Matthew was seven,
He decided to leave home.
He packed his little bag
And tucked his teddy underneath his arm,
And said, "I'm going, I've had enough."
"Why are you leaving, Matty?" asked Dad.
"Because you shouted at me."
"No I didn't. I never raised my voice."
"You shouted at me with your eyes," said Matthew.
"Shall I run you to the station?" asked Dad.
"No, I'll get a bus."
"Well, goodbye then, Matty," said Dad, opening the door
On to the cold, black night beyond.
Matthew peered into the darkness.
"And be careful of the wolves," said Dad.
"I'm not going now," replied Matthew.
"I've changed my mind."

Gervase Phinn

One evening I was called in by the Mother Superior of the children's home. She was a strict lady and I thought I was going to be in for some kind of telling off.

"Have a seat, my child," she said.

Then she started talking about being sent to Australia. Blimey, I thought, have I been that bad to be sent away?

Mother Superior went on to say that I had been chosen, that it was a wonderful opportunity, not some kind of punishment. But that night in bed, I cried. I was so frightened of leaving the only home I'd ever had, of leaving my school friends, my only sisters, of leaving my best friend Pearl, and never seeing any of them again.

anonymous

Gold medals are like children, you don't

It was in your teens that you really started to adopt a hairstyle and dictate how you wanted it cutting and shaping. You often saw notices outside shops stating 'Army haircuts repaired', and there was a shortage of suitable hairdressing during my austerity-ridden youth.

John Morgan

He gazed and gazed and gazed and gazed,
Amazed, amazed, amazed, amazed.

Robert Browning,
'Rhyme for a Child Viewing a Naked Venus
in a Painting of the Judgement of Paris'

After tea, the bright boys wash, clean their boots, and change into their 'second-best' attire, and stroll forth ... in company with others, up and down that parade until they 'click' with one of the 'birds'. The girls are out on much the same pro-gramme. They, too, promenade until they 'click' with some-one, and are escorted to a picture palace or hall or chocolate shop ... As the boys pass the likely girls they glance, and, if not rebuffed, offer wide smiles. But they do not stop. At the sec-ond meeting, however, they smile again and touch hands in passing, or cry over the shoulder some current witticism, as "Snice night, Ethel!" or "I should shay sho!" And Ethel and Lucy will swing around, challengingly, with scraping feet, and cry, "Oooh!" The boys linger at the corner, looking back, and the girls, too, look back. Ethel asks Lucy, "Shall we?" and Lucy says, "Ooh — I do," and by the time the boys have come down level with them ... "Well — shall we stroll 'cross the Common?" "I don't mind." Then boys and girls move forward together ... They have 'got off'.

Clapham Common in 1915

have a favourite. Sir Steve Redgrave

One cherished fragment of sex-lore amongst our group was that any Belgian or French girl student who wore a gold cross on a chain was easy game. Easy game for what was not clear to us younger members of the group, but we cried, "Yes, aren't they!" and leered along with the big boys.

Frank Muir

One boy "knew for a fact" that women were unable to lift their arms above their heads owing to the formation of their breasts; you couldn't count javelin-throwers because they'd had operations. None of the others could remember a mother or sister actually raising her arms that high, so they made an expedition to the village shop, where a young women worked, and asked for something off a high shelf. She got a stepladder and climbed up so that she didn't have to reach above her head. The authoritative boy had his credibility confirmed.

Alan Ayckbourn

We tried to get the girls to play in the wood and in various barns and sheds with limited success and often they declined our many thinly veiled invitations.

John Iveson

The parson told us not to do it, the doctor told us not to do it, and the headmaster told us where not to do it.

anonymous

ITMA set a pattern for romantic lads and lasses who posted letters with SWALK — 'sealed with a loving kiss' — on the back of the envelope. HOLLAND — 'hope our love lasts and never dies' — was another, and others used BOLTOP with a line of kisses. It meant 'better on lips than on paper'. Shyness prevents me from explaining the meaning of BURMA.

John Morgan

Few things are more satisfying than seeing your children

have teenagers of their own. Doug Larson

By twelve I had a good idea where babies came from, but until I started secondary school and the big boys 'educated' me, I was pretty naïve. Of course, like all boys, I bluffed.

I was ten years old and wandering around Broom Valley Junior School yard one sunny lunchtime with Jimmy Everett and Terry Gaunt, my best pals, when Roy Evans sidled up.

"Guess what?"

"What?" we chorused.

"My next door neighbour's lass, Soppy Sandra, is up t' spout!"

There were many descriptions of pregnancy and Roy knew the whole dictionary of them — 'up the spout', 'in the pudding club', 'a bun in the oven', 'in the family way', 'up the duff', 'eating for two'.

"Oh," we replied, trying to sound uninterested.

"S'right. There was a right old row last night when 'er old man found out. You should have 'eard 'em shouting. All t' street could 'ear. Soppy Sandra were roaring 'er eyes out, 'er old man were blowing 'is top and 'er old woman were tellin' 'em both to shurrup cos all t' neighbours could 'ear. It were great."

"She should have been more careful," said Terry, sounding like his father.

Roy tried to impress us. "You can't get pregnant, tha knows, if t' bloke 'as an 'ot shower before he does it."

"We know that!" snapped Jimmy, as ignorant as I was.

"But you can if you swim too close to somebody at t' swimming baths and they pee in t' watter," said Terry.

"And if you put your tongue in their mouth when tha's snoggin' — that's a sure way," added Jimmy, chancing his arm.

"Or have a bath after somebody," declared Roy confidently, not wishing to be outdone by the other two experts.

"Who told thee that?" asked Terry, fascinated.

"Our kid." Roy winked. "He's cooartin, tha knaws."

Children aren't happy with nothing to ignore,

I had remained silent, and then three pairs of eyes turned in my direction.

"Have you been told t' facts o' life then, Phinny?" asked Roy.

"Course I have," I lied, attempting to sound blasé. "My dad told me last year."

Gervase Phinn

Mum also noticed around this time that I had begun to open my eyes to the possibility that girls might offer more than pig-tails to pull. When I came home one day and announced casually that I required some Lifebuoy soap, Mum's response was immediate.

"What's her name?" she inquired.

"Margaret," I told her.

"And what is the attraction?"

"She can run faster than me."

Ian Botham

I'd make sly, tentative trysts with girls from next door, but we didn't really know what to do with them except sort of stand there. The streetwise butcher boy would have made his way through most of the girls in the village and I was still wondering whether to ask them out.

Alan Ayckbourn

As I recall these childhood memories in a farming community, my later interest in biology and bacteriology may have its beginnings — in Pa standing with me at the gate while a stallion performed its male duties. Subsequently when the foal arrived I was convinced that calves came from father horses and mother cows — an innocent thought later put right when we acquired a farm bull.

John Iveson

And that's what parents were created for. Ogden Nash

The child is father of the man; And I could wish my days and years to be,

If I were to pinpoint a single moment when I began to notice girls, it would be on this holiday. Which ones had bumps on their chests? Which ones didn't? Who had the nicest curves and the prettiest smile? Up until then I knew they were different, but only because they smelled nicer and didn't fight so much.

My entire life changed. I had a mission. The nightly games in Lance Street reflected this. Suddenly the aim was to catch a girl and kiss her, instead of running the other way.

We didn't have dates as such. Instead we found a dark corner and hoped to steal a kiss or perhaps a little more.

That's when I made my next important discovery. The other lads were trying to impress girls by boasting or fighting, but I had more success making them laugh and feel good about themselves.

Ricky Tomlinson

What is not in doubt is young Henry Moore's interest in the opposite sex, and especially in the contours of the female form. In the morning assembly, for example, the girls stood in front of the boys.

"If their bodies and features had been hidden by a board below which only their legs showed from the knees down, I could still have given a name to each pair."

Roger Berthoud

We had something called 'health lessons' which seemed to consist of instructions on how to clean your teeth and cut your nails. There was certainly no sex education, although we boys and girls who sat in the back row had our own lessons which consisted of "I'll show you mine if you show me yours".

Virginia Watkinson

Bound each to each by natural piety. William Wordsworth

It was in the middle of an arithmetic lesson that I discovered the enormous satisfaction that came from creating laughter and it became the main aim of my working life.

I was sitting at a double desk with a plump fellow scholar who was almost asleep with boredom. To cheer him up I made a humorous remark. He sniggered and whispered what I had said to the boy behind him and he sniggered too.

Mr Rule's fat fairy forefinger bent in a beckoning movement and I slid out from my desk and stood next to him, clutching my pencil, knuckles white with fear.

"Muir, you were talking in class again. That is not permitted, heh? Vill you kindly repeat aloud vat you said to Leatherbarrow? It is fair, is it not, that you share your vit vith all of us?"

"Please, sir," I mumbled, "I said, 'This pencil top is sir's bum'."

The roomfull of children erupted in joyful mirth. It was an intoxicating moment. I had made the whole school laugh.

It might be thought that it was not really much of a joke on which to base a career. It was not even remotely witty, but the roomful of children laughed at what I had said and my destiny was fixed.

Frank Muir

There is this incredible need to perform in front of people and I've had it since I was six years of age.

Ernie Wise

At that stage it [*Reluctant Heroes*] was just about the funniest play I'd ever read. The evening up till then had been rather turgid and this was just sensationally successful. People were standing and cheering and I just thought "I've just got to wait here and say this line and I know it'll happen. This is just giddy-making." I remember thinking how glad I was on

We find delight in the beauty and happiness of children that

Monday I was starting serious theatre. I'd felt what it was like to have an audience in the palm of my hand — for twenty-five minutes at most. Although it was to be redirected, that was quite an influential moment in my life.

Alan Ayckbourn

I never really wanted to be a performer. I had bright ambitions. To me my future was clear. At fifteen I would get myself a paper round. At seventeen I would learn to read it. And at eighteen I would get a job on the corporation like my dad.

Eric Morecambe

I felt completely at home the first time I went on stage, at the age of twelve. It's my job and it's where I look forward to being.

Patrick Stewart

When I was a child all the grown-ups around me had a joke, that is to say, all the women grown-ups. If we passed a pair of lovers spooning on a park bench my mother would look significantly at my Aunt Winnie, and Aunt Winnie would say, "Life with a capital 'L'," and they would both laugh secretly and I would feel uncomfortable.

If we passed a gaudy lady on the street my aunt would look significantly at my mother and my mother would say, "Life, etc," and they would both laugh and I would look at the lady and my mother would say, 'Don't look, Charlie. She's a theatrical!'

I remember the incident because the gaudy lady was dressed in white, with a white parasol and pink roses on her hat, and my mother nearly yanked my arm out of its socket and I became an actor. I suppose by now you've got the idea.

Charles Laughton

makes the heart too big for the body. Ralph Waldo Emerson

The sound of all those voices in that setting was unbelievable. But it used to irritate me when people did things badly. When I began to sing in these choirs — I was a high soprano at the time — it annoyed me if somebody next to me did not seem to know what to do with a musical phrase. I was probably a very nasty and arrogant little girl, but the thing was inborn: until then I had no musical training.

Janet Barber

Childhood

What do I remember of the bygone days?
Little of the sorrow, something of the praise.

Pleasant games of childhood, in the pleasant shade,
Toiling at a pleasure, playing at a trade!

Often very weary, never glad to rest.
Taking love and laughter with a reckless zest.

Claiming, howso heedless, still to be approved;
Cold to those that loved me, wroth with those I loved.

Now that I am older, what is left behind?
Still I take, unthankful, service, love, delight.
Laugh to see the morning, murmur at the night.

Do I doubt Thy goodness, question of Thy will?
Father, Lord, forgive us — we are children still.

Arthur Christopher Benson

I have often thought what a melancholy world this

would be without children. Samuel Taylor Coleridge

The first professional play Judi Dench saw was lighter fare —
Ben Travers' farce *Cuckoo in the Nest* at the York Theatre
Royal:

"I can never forget when a man appeared in long johns
from a basket at the bottom of a bed. I screamed with laughter so much that my parents took me home because they
thought I'd make myself ill.

"But Ma did take me again the next night to see the rest of the
play, which was very tolerant of her. I can still clearly remember that place. It was cleaned with something like Jeyes Fluid,
and a string trio played from the pit. Even now I can evoke
that particular smell, and hear that unique sound of the trio."

John Miller

I read every book that came in my way without distinction —
and my father was very fond of me and used to take me on his
knee, and hold long conversations with me. I remember, that
at eight years old I walked with him one winter evening from
a farmer's house, a mile from Ottery — and he told me the
names of the stars — and how Jupiter was a thousand times
larger than our world — and that the other twinkling stars
were Suns that had worlds rolling round them and when I
came home, he shewed me how they rolled round — I heard
him with a profound delight and admiration; but without the
least mixture of wonder or incredulity. For from my early
reading of Faery Tales and Genii etc etc — my mind had had
habituated to the Vast.

Samuel Taylor Coleridge

Are all young children naturally dishonest? I've often
pondered this question, for in my young days most of us were.
Yet I think most of us grew up to be reasonably good citizens
and certainly not dishonest.

C T Maltby

It is not a bad thing that children should occasionally,

The Lesson

"Your father's gone," my bald headmaster said.
His shiny dome and brown tobacco jar
Splintered at once in tears. It wasn't grief.
I cried for knowledge which was bitterer
Than any grief. For there and then I knew
That grief has uses — that a father dead
Could bind the bully's fist a week or two;
And then I cried for shame, then for relief.

I was a month past ten when I learnt this:
I still remember how the noise was stilled
In school-assembly when my grief came in.
Some goldfish in a bowl quietly sculled
Around their shining prison on its shelf.
They were indifferent. All the other eyes
Were turned towards me. Somewhere in myself
Pride, like a goldfish, flashed a sudden fin.

Edward Lucie-Smith

All gone; except in my head. There, the old world lives on as
vivid now as it was then, but the young wouldn't recognise it
and the rest of the world thinks it is a joke.

Austin Mitchell MP

I have flashbacks to those days, as I do from time to time.
The first picture reflects the warmth and comfort of our
surroundings, the feeling of being wanted and safe. I'll say it
again — no child can be given anything more valuable than
that by his or her parents.

Brian Clough

---

and politely, put parents in their place. Colette

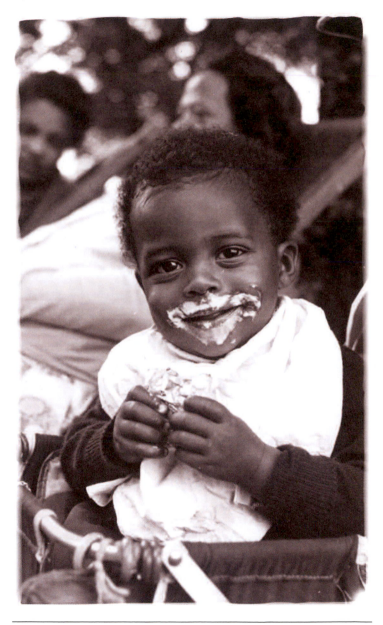

Children are a gift from the Lord:

Good Parents

(Parody in answer to Philip Larkin)

They tuck you in, good parents do,
They kiss your cheek and hold you tight,
They fill your world with gentle dreams
And pray you'll have a peaceful night.

For they were tucked in, in their turn
By mums and dads who loved them so,
And by such loving quickly learnt
To love their children as they grow.

Good parents hand such happiness on,
It's endless like the sky above,
So learn this lesson parents do,
And teach your children how to love.

Gervase Phinn

they are a real blessing. The Bible, Psalm 127

Acknowledgements

The author and publishers would like to thank the following for permission to reproduce material. All text and photographs are © the contributors unless indicated otherwise. Every effort has been made to track down copyright holders. The publishers would be pleased to receive details of any errors and omissions, to be corrected in subsequent editions.

p3: 'The first thing...', Graham Greene, *A Sort of Life* (Vintage Books); 'We were a happy family...', © 1998 Graham McCann, *Morecambe & Wise* (HarperCollins Ltd); 'Insignificant is not a word...', Brian Clough, *Cloughie: Walking on Water* (Headline, 2002); 'The smell...', from *Dear Tom* by Tom Courtenay, published by Doubleday, reproduced by permission of the Random House Group Ltd; 'The Mitchells...', Austin Mitchell ('What it Means to be Yorkshire', *Yorkshire Journal* autumn 1999); 'Mexborough...', David Morgan Rees ('Memories of a Mexborough Butcher's Boy', *Yorkshire Journal* summer 1993); **p5**: 'Apart from...', © Geoffrey Boycott, *Boycott* (Pan Macmillan, London, 1987); 'I was...', Charles Chaplin, *My Autobiography* (Random House, 1964); 'I can remember...', Martin Cluderay, 'Memories of Leeds in the Twenties' (*Yorkshire Journal* spring 1997); **p6**: 'My mother's thrift...', Stan Barstow, *In My Own Good Time* (Smith Settle, 2001); 'Fish and chips...', Austin Mitchell, ibid; 'We ate...', © 1998 Graham McCann, ibid; 'When at home...', Mrs Gaskell, *The Life of Charlotte Brontë*; **p7**: 'Growing up...', Maeve Binchy (*Guardian*, 29.10.2003); 'Children...', George A Jarratt (*Dalesman* vol 20); 'I remember...', Irene Abrahams, *When I Was a Child* (Victoire Press, 2007); **p8**: 'A favourite...', from *A Kentish Lad* by Frank Muir, published by Bantam Press, reprinted by permission of the Random House Group Ltd; 'At Woodhead...', John Morgan, *Morgan's Yorkshire* (Smith Settle, 2000); 'Penny Ducks...' David Morgan Rees; **p10**: 'My father...', E M J Reid (*Dalesman* vol 21); 'We used to...', John Iveson (*Dalesman*); 'The railway came...', Janice Sinson, 'A Whitby Childhood' (*Yorkshire Journal* winter 2001); 'One Friday...', May Crewe (*Dalesman* vol 13); **p11**: 'Every day...', Anna Davin, *Growing Up Poor* (Rivers Oram Press, 1996); 'At twelve...', I Greaves (*Dalesman* vol 12); 'I was born...', J Fairfax Blakeborough (*Dalesman* vol 2); **p13**: 'It was...', John Iveson, ibid; 'Although...', Hazel Mary Martell, personal contribution; 'Nobody doubted...', Roy Hattersley, *A Yorkshire Boyhood* (Little Brown, 2003); **p14**: 'My friend...', Stan Barstow, ibid; 'We had...', © Fred Trueman, *As it Was* (Pan Macmillan, London, 2004); 'Mam kept an eye...', Brian Clough, ibid; 'I always think...', Janice Sinson, ibid; **p17**: 'The day...', George Sweeting, 'They Matter' (*Yorkshire Journal* no037); 'In many ways...', © Geoffrey Boycott, ibid; **p19**: 'I remember...', George Sweeting, ibid; 'I told...', Stephen Spender, (*The Old School*, ed Graham Greene, Cape, 1934); **p20**: 'My father...', Blake Morrison, *And When Did You Last See Your Father?* (Granta Books, 1997); 'A Dalesman...', © Gervase Phinn 2008;

p23: 'They were...', John Morgan, ibid; 'I was...', © Fred Trueman, ibid; 'When I was...', W M Hudson (*Dalesman* vol 22); **p24**: 'Eggs are...', John Morgan, ibid; 'I remember...', Nicholas Charles (*Dalesman* vol 20); 'My father...', Blake Morrison, ibid; 'In the 1950s...', Hazel Martell, ibid; **p25**: 'Dad was tall...', Frank Muir, ibid; 'The pièce-de-resistance...', E M J Reid, ibid; 'He was...', Roger Berthoud, *A Life of Henry Moore* (Giles de la Mere Publishers, 2003); **p26**: 'In his...', Linda Pollock, *A Lasting Relationship* (University Press of New England); 'I loved my dad...', Ricky Tomlinson, *Ricky* (Little Brown Book Group, 2003); 'Dad would bring...', Martin Cluderay, ibid; 'Dad hadn't...', Nicholas Charles, ibid; **p27**: 'Worldly rationalist...', Blake Morrison, ibid; 'My proudest moment...', © Fred Trueman, ibid; 'I would...', © Geoffrey Boycott, ibid; 'My father...', Stan Barstow, ibid; **p28**: 'Our parents'...', George A Jarratt, ibid; 'My mother...', John Morgan, ibid; 'When my mother...', © Fred Trueman, ibid; 'I was...', Tom Courtenay, ibid; **p30**: 'A wise mother...', Oliver Greenwood (*Dalesman* vol 21); 'Piano', D H Lawrence, *Collected Poems of D H Lawrence* (Martin Secker, 1929); '[My mother]...', Roger Berthoud, ibid; 'Mother...', May Crewe, ibid; 'I recall...', John Chippendale, 'A Simple and Contented Life' (*Yorkshire Journal* autumn 1997); 'Fragments...', George Sweeting, ibid; 'A Parent's Prayer', © Gervase Phinn 2008; **p35**: 'I think...', Ricky Tomlinson, ibid; **p36**: 'Childhood' by Frances Cornford is from her *Selected Poems* (Enitharmon Press, 1996); 'There was...', Nicholas Charles, ibid; 'I can locate...', Stan Barstow, ibid; **p37**: 'My Granddad', Dora Berry (*Yorkshire Journal* no41); **p38**: 'Grandpa Bain', Vernon Scannell (*Yorkshire Journal* winter 2001); 'I remember...', George Sweeting, ibid; 'My younger brother...', © Geoffrey Boycott, ibid; **p40**: 'I liked...', Stan Barstow, ibid; 'Grandma Quest...', Tom Courtenay, ibid; 'On one...', Nicholas Charles, ibid; **p41**: 'Our family...', Austin Mitchell MP, ibid; 'My girlfriend's...', C Metalfe, personal contribution; 'My most vivid...', Nicholas Charles; ibid; 'We visited...', Richard Riley, personal contribution; 'Grandma Quest...', Tom Courtenay, ibid; **p42**: 'Our neighbour...', John Morgan, ibid; 'Nothing...', E M J Reid, ibid; **p44**: 'Cricket...', © Geoffrey Boycott, ibid; 'Uncle Stow...', Janice Sinson, ibid; **p45**: 'My brothers...', Elizabeth Collingwood (*Dalesman* vol 23); 'When Mam...', Nicholas Charles, ibid; 'Auntie Maud...', John Morgan, ibid; 'We stayed...', Richard Riley, ibid; **p46**: 'There was...', Frank Muir, ibid; 'Aunt Eliza...', John Morgan, ibid; 'My sister...', Elizabeth Collingwood, ibid; 'My cousin...', Hazel Martell, ibid; **p47**: 'A lot...', Janice Sinson, ibid; **p49**: 'Notwithstanding...', John Bunyan, Selected Works; 'About Five...', Thomas Tryon, *Social History* no4; 'My first day...', Pauline Molineaux, personal contribution; **p50**: 'I started...', Hazel Martell, ibid; **p51**:'On my...', Norene Walbridge, personal contribution; 'School...', Adam Martindale, The Life of Adam Martindale (Chetham Society, 1845); 'Think...', Charles Lamb, *Letters vol I* (Methuen, 1904); 'I was...', Graham McCann, ibid; 'A friend...', John Mortimer, Clinging to the Wreckage (Weidenfeld & Nicolson, an imprint of the Orion Publishing Group); 'If public school...' Paul Allen, *Grinning at the Edge: A Biography of Alan Ayckbourn* (Methuen, 2001); **p52**: 'I had...', Frank Taylor, *Wit of the Classroom* (Frewin, 1972); 'I was...', James Fretwell, *Social*

History no4; 'I found...', *Dalesman*; **p53**: 'When he can talk...', John Locke, *Collected Works* (1882); 'Our uniforms...', Fred Vermorel, Fashion & Perversity: The Life of Vivien Westwood (Bloomsbury, 1994); 'I wasn't...', Graham McCann, ibid; 'He has...', Frank Taylor, ibid; **p54**: 'It's true...', Diane Taylor, 'Gypsy voices' (Guardian, August 2003); **p55**: 'In 1899...', S E Raistrick, 'A Dales Schoolmaster' (*Dalesman* vol 21); 'None...', Janice Sinson, ibid; 'My stay...', Stan Barstow, ibid; **p57**: 'I was...', Humphries, *Hooligans & Rebels* (Wiley & Sons); 'I told...', Roger Berthoud, ibid; 'Mam and Dad...', Tom Courtenay, ibid; **p58**: 'We were...', Austin Mitchell MP, ibid; 'I must...', Wood & Thompson, *Personal Recollections of the Twentieth Century* (BBC Books, 1993); 'The School Meals...', Joan Walkland (Dalesman 1962); **p61**: 'A tuck box...', Road Dahl, *Boy* (Jonathan Cape & Penguin Books Ltd, 1983); 'He has...', Frank Taylor, ibid; 'When I was...', Linda Pollock, *Lasting Relationship* (Fourth Estate, 1987); **p62**: 'Judi...', Frank Taylor, ibid; 'All this while...', Thomas Tryon, *Social History*; **p64**: 'Village School', Margaret Jones (*Dalesman* vol 23); **p66**: 'The schoolmaster...', S E Raistrick, ibid; 'A Child of the Dales', © Gervase Phinn 2008; **p67**: 'From the age...', William Stout, *Autobiography* (Chetham Society, 1852); 'At country schools...', Richard Baxter; 'It became...', Paul Allen, ibid; 'There were...', John Iveson, ibid; 'Boys from...', *The Life & Death of Thomas a Becket*; 'I spent...', Graham McCann, ibid; **p68**: 'I was...', Arthur Kitching (*Yorkshire Journal* no 43); 'I never...', Dirk Bogarde, *A Postillion Struck by Lightning* (Orion Books, 1977); 'The lighthouse...', George A Jarratt (*Dalesman*); 'There were...', Geoff Townsend, personal contribution; **p70**: 'My education...', Charles Shaw, *When I Was a Child* (1903); 'I never...', Nicholas Murray, Andrew Marvell (Abacus, 1999); 'The affairs...', courtesy Gervase Phinn; **p71**: 'Attention...', courtesy Gervase Phinn; 'We had...', Elizabeth Collingwood, ibid; 'On returning...', Norene Walbridge, personal contribution; **p72**: 'The teaching...', Stan Barstow, ibid; 'The most...', Tom Courtenay, ibid; 'Away from...', © Fred Trueman, ibid; **p73**: 'My primary...', Alan Blythe, *Janet Barber* (Ian Allen, 1973); 'I could read...', Mavis Holt, personal contribution; 'Schooldays...', © Geoffrey Boycott, ibid; **p74**: 'He shows...', Frank Taylor, ibid; 'I loved...', Elizabeth Collingwood, ibid; 'The person...', Ruth Newey, personal contribution; 'The teacher...', Graham McCann; 'A talkative...', John Iveson, ibid; 'The boy...', Frank Taylor, ibid; **p76**: 'Remembering...', © Gervase Phinn 2008; **p77**: 'The cane...', John Morgan, ibid; 'The archaic...', © Stephen Berkoff, non-attributed excerpt of Stephen Berkoff's reproduce by kind permission of Rosica Collin Limited, London; 'Constantly...', Frank Taylor, ibid; 'On second thoughts...', William Taylor (Dalesman vol 22); **p79**: 'I remember...', John Iveson, ibid; 'And when...', Pinchbeck & Hewitt, *Children in English Society* (1969); **p80**: 'The one...', Tom Courtenay, ibid; 'Don't...', Frank Taylor, ibid; 'Some people...', ©Fred Trueman, ibid; **p82**: 'As a child...', courtesy John Morgan; 'The worlde...', *vulgaria*, Magdalene College, Oxford; **p83**: 'Remember Me?', © Gervase Phinn 2008; 'My lasting...', Robert Graves, *Goodbye to all That* (1929); **p87**: 'A pub...', Frank Muir, ibid; 'The memory...', H E Bates, *The Vanished World* (Methuen Publishing, 1969); 'I never...', Gilliam Peak, *When I Was a Child*, ibid; **p88**: 'I was proud...', Graham McCann, ibid; 'If variety...', Mrs M Heath (*Dalesman* vol 20); 'When...', Roy Hattersley, ibid; 'The first memory...', Mavis Holt, ibid; **p91**: 'The rabbit...', D H Lawrence, *Phoenix: Posthumous Papers*, courtesy Pollinger Ltd; 'I wish...', Pollock, ibid; 'He was...', Roger Berthoud, ibid; 'We would...', Richard Riley, personal contribution; **p92**: 'Eche time...', Alexander Barclay, *Eclogues*; 'Between five...', Professor Richard Hoggart, *The Uses of Literacy* (Random House, *1957*); **p94**: 'The Ecchoing Green', William Blake, *Complete Poems*; **p95**: 'One of...', Richard Riley, personal contribution; 'St Cuthbert...', Venerable Bede, *The Biography of St Cuthbert*; 'When mere...', Elizabeth Gaskell, ibid; 'When the other...', Gerald of Wales, *Autobiography*; 'Girls...', Malcolm Andrews, 'Childhood'; 'My brothers'...', Pollock, ibid; 'I remember...', John Townsend (*Dalesman* vol 22); 'Ma and Pa...', John Iveson, ibid; 'Taken...', Paul Allen, ibid; **p98**: 'The railway...', Frank Muir, ibid; 'My father...', John Chippendale, 'A Beekeeping Boyhood' (*Yorkshire Journal* summer 1998); 'In my...', Ruth Hedger (*Dalesman* vol 21); **p100**: 'Dad was...', Nicholas Charles, ibid; 'Christmas was...', Hilary Shields (*Yorkshire Journal* winter 1996); **p102**: 'Shortly before...', John Chippendale, ibid; 'I have...', © Fred Trueman, ibid; **p103**: 'Then...', © Melvyn Bragg, *Rich: the life of Richard Burton*, reproduced by permission of Hodder & Stoughton Ltd; **p105**: 'Everyone...', Dinah C M Brown, personal contribution; 'I loved...', Sir Bernard Ingham, 'My Yorkshire Boyhood' (*Yorkshire Journal* no41); 'When...', J A Barringer (*Dalesman* vol 6); **p106**: 'Bonfire Night', © Gervase Phinn 2008; 'There was...', Eva Wise (*Dalesman* vol 15); **p107**: 'The local...', John Miller, *Judi Dench: With a Crack in Her Voice* (Weidenfeld & Nicolson, an imprint of the Orion Publishing Group, 1998); '"How I wish"...', Molly Hughes, *A London Child of the 1870s*; 'The young people...', Mabel Horner Thompson (*Dalesman* vol 13); **p108**: 'It is difficult...', Fiona Pitt-Kethley, *My Schooling* (Tamworth Press); 'I remember...', Ricky Tomlinson, ibid; 'September 1939...', Mavis Holt, ibid; **p110**: 'There was...', John Morgan, ibid; 'In spring...', Sir Bernard Ingham, ibid; 'There was...', John Iveson, ibid; **p111**: 'The back gardens...', © Geoffrey Boycott, ibid; 'Taws...', John Morgan, ibid; 'Looking back...', J Laycock (*Dalesman* vol 6); **p113**: 'A game...', John Morgan, ibid; 'Gaffers...', J A Barringer, ibid; 'Thirty years ago...', R M Chapman (Dalesman vol 1); **p114**: 'Lads' hobbies...', Ian Dewhirst (*Yorkshire Journal*); **p115**: 'When I was...', John Morgan, ibid; 'Give me...', Samuel Taylor Coleridge, *Collected Works*; 'Being...', © Fred Trueman, ibid; **p116**: 'In imitation...', Thomas Bewick, *A Memoir*; 'In late summer...', Sir Bernard Ingham, ibid; 'We got...', Hazell Martell, ibid; 'As far as...', © Fred Trueman, ibid; **p117**: 'I can't...', Janice Sinson, ibid; 'As a boy...', Patrick Stewart (*Yorkshire Journal*); 'For us...', Austin Mitchell MP, ibid; 'Inspired...', Ricky Tomlinson, ibid; 'For the...', Tony Law, personal contribution; **p118**: 'In keeping with ...', Frank Muir, ibid; 'One of...', Ricky Tomlinson, ibid; **p119**: 'There was...', Austin Mitchell MP, ibid; 'At chapel...', John Iveson, ibid; 'The vocal...', Frank Muir, ibid; 'When my brother...', Richard Riley, personal contribution; 'As a child...', Rebecca Hey (*Dalesman* vol 14); **p122**: 'But the memories...', Arthur Ransome, by permission of the Arthur Ransome Literary Estate; 'Adolf Hitler...', Ricky

Tomlinson, ibid; 'Once I had…', © Ian Botham 1994, *Botham: My Autobiography* (HarperCollins Publishers Ltd); **p123**: 'Infant Joy', William Blake, ibid; 'When my children…', Elizabeth Gaskell, ibid; 'My earliest…', Mavis Holt, ibid; 'Most people…', John Holt, *Escape from Childhood* (Holt Associates Inc); **p126**: 'Childhood Dream', Will Clemence (*Dalesman* vol 12); 'Wakes…', John Morgan, ibid; **p128**: 'On and off…', Henry Mayhew, *London Labour & the London Poor* (1850); 'I am…', Florence Warren, *The Dance of Death* (1931); **p129**: 'We children…', Mabel Horner Thompson, ibid; 'We were…', Jeremy Seabrook, *Working-Class Childhood* (Gollancz, 1982); 'If there is…', © Fred Trueman, ibid; 'It surprised me…', Richard Riley, ibid; **p131**: 'My love…', Frank Muir, ibid; 'Children…', Phil May, *Gutter-snipes* (1896); 'We weren't…', June Rose, *For the Sake of the Children* (Hodder & Stoughton Ltd, 1987); **p132**: 'Leaving Home', © Gervase Phinn 2008; 'One evening…', Bean & Melville, *Lost Children of the Empire* (Harper-Collins Publishers Ltd, 1989); **p133**: 'It was…', John Morgan, ibid; 'He gazed…', Robert Browning, *Collected Poems*; 'After tea…', © John Gills, *For Better or Worse: British Marriage 1600 to Present* (1986), by permission of Oxford University Press Inc; **p134**: 'One cherished…', Frank Muir, ibid; 'One boy…', Paul Allen, ibid; 'We tried…', John Iveson; 'The parson…', Frank Taylor; ibid; 'ITMA…', John Morgan; ibid; **p136**: 'By twelve…', © Gervase Phinn 2008; **p137**: 'Mum also noticed…', © Ian Botham, ibid; 'I'd make…', Paul Allen, ibid; 'As I recall…', John Iveson, ibid; **p139**: 'If I were…', Ricky Tomlinson, ibid; 'What is not…', Roger Berthoud, ibid; 'We had…', Virginia Watkinson, *When I Was a Child*; **p140**: 'It was…', Frank Muir, ibid; 'There is…', Graham McCann, ibid; 'At that stage…', Paul Allen, ibid; 'I never…', Graham McCann, ibid; 'I felt…', Patrick Stewart, ibid; 'When I was…', Simon Callow, *Charles Laughton: a difficult actor* (Methuen, 1987); **p142**: 'The sound…', Alan Blyth, ibid; 'Childhood', A C Benson, *Collected Works*; **p144**: 'The first…', John Miller, ibid; 'I read…' S T Coleridge, ibid; 'Are all…', C T Maltby, ibid; **p145**: 'The Lesson', copyright © Edward Lucie-Smith, reproduced by permission of the author c/o Rogers, Coleridge & White Ltd, 20 Powis Mews, London W11 1JN; 'All gone…', Austin Mitchell MP, ibid; 'I have flashbacks…', Brian Clough, ibid; **p147**: 'Parents', © Gervase Phinn 2008.

Photographic acknowledgements: Ian Dewhirst, p114; A J Halliday, p127; Hulton Archive, pp4, 9, 12,15, 16, 21, 22, 29, 31, 39, 47, 56, 59, 60, 63, 65, 69, 75, 78, 81, 89, 90, 93, 96, 99, 101, 104, 109, 112, 125, 130, 135, 138, 143, 146; Tom Parker, p54; Gervase Phinn, frontispiece, pp35, 50, 52, 85, 86.